Justice in Taxation

Robert G. Kennedy

ACTON INSTITUTE

Christian Social Thought Series
Number 25 • Edited by Kevin Schmiesing

Christian Social Thought Series, Number 25

Cover image: Money Balance
Source: www.istock.com.

ISBN: 978-1-942503-72-9

Interior composition: Judy Schafer
Cover: Peter Ho

ACTONINSTITUTE

98 E. Fulton
Grand Rapids, Michigan 49503
616.454.3080
www.acton.org

Printed in the United States of America

Contents

Foreword

As Professor Kennedy observes in his introduction, the topic here addressed is a perennial one in human experience. The moral conundrums that taxation presents to Christians were evident even in the time of Christ, when Pharisees tried to entrap Jesus with a subtle question concerning whether to pay the duties levied by Caesar (Matt. 20:15–22).

Neither the state nor the economy has gotten any smaller or simpler since the first century, but the teachings of the Gospel remain relevant to those who are today striving to live as disciples of Jesus in all aspects of their lives, including their engagement of economics and politics. As Kennedy shows, the Catholic social tradition provides a rich resource on which to draw as we continue to reflect on the rights and obligations of individuals, families, associations, businesses, and governments. Kennedy's learned, thorough, and even-handed treatment of taxation in the light of Catholic thought and teaching raises the important questions and clarifies the important issues with respect to the morality of taxation.

As with many topics within Catholic social teaching, the virtues of justice and prudence are indispensable tools in our efforts to assess and generate tax policies that truly serve the good of all. Happily, Kennedy displays the same virtues as he recounts the history of taxation, analyzes its moral dimensions, and considers the merits and demerits of contemporary theories and practices. Following the tradition, he recognizes the state's role in society and justifies its collection of revenue to support its proper functions. But he also does justice to the Church's emphasis on the dignity of the person, the centrality of the family, and the indispensable role of the institutions of civil society—an emphasis that places limits on the state's tendency to widen its scope and extend its grasp. With its well-rounded enunciation of the moral obligations pertaining to all parties—individuals, associations, and governments—this book enables us to take a large first step toward formulating tax policies that are both and sensible and ethical.

Kevin Schmiesing
Acton Institute

Acknowledgments

Any scholar is dependent on the work of those who went before. In working on this topic, I benefited from the thoughtful work of economists, accountants, historians, political scientists, philosophers, and theologians. In particular, though, I would like to acknowledge the assistance of two experts in taxation. Tim Rademacher, a member of the accounting faculty in the Opus College of Business at the University of St. Thomas, clarified some technical points for me and was kind enough to lend me some materials that provided further resources for my work. My friend John Kelly, senior vice president for tax at a large corporation, listened graciously to some of my early ideas and was very helpful in acquainting me with some of the strategies employed to mitigate corporate tax obligations. His professional integrity assisted me to see where lines might be drawn between adroit and abusive behaviors. I have also appreciated the work of Dr. Kevin Schmiesing, the general editor of this series for the Acton Institute. He suggested this project to me and patiently waited for me to produce a draft long after his initial deadline had passed. His gentle and careful editing has made it a better book.

This volume is dedicated to my friend and mentor, Germain Grisez (1929–2018), who passed to his eternal reward as this book was in final preparation.

Part I

Principles of Catholic Social Teaching

1 Introduction

In a letter written in 1789, Benjamin Franklin observed that the new American constitution seemed destined for permanency but also noted that "in this world nothing can be said to be certain, except death and taxes." Taxation, in one form or another, has been a feature of civilized life for five thousand years or more and shows no sign of disappearing. No doubt complaints about the fairness of taxation are just as old.

In general, my objective for this volume is to consider questions of justice with regard to taxation through the lens of the Catholic social tradition. This immediately presents some challenges. The field of taxation necessarily is an intersection of a number of perspectives: politics, economics, law, accounting, and even philosophy and theology. As such, it offers a range of complications not usually found in other areas of applied ethics.

A second challenge, which is only too common in applied ethics, has to do with the number of competing, and incompatible, ethical theories that are brought to bear on practical questions. As Alasdair MacIntyre pointed out in *After Virtue*, modern ethicists often use the same words and phrases, many borrowed from classical philosophy, but they attach very different meanings to them. As a consequence, for example, philosophers (to say nothing of economists and legal scholars) argue earnestly about the *justice* of particular tax policies, but they often do so with very different understandings of precisely what they mean by the term. It would be hard to say that they disagree with one another because disagreement implies at least some common understanding of the matter at hand.

Rather than describing the principal approaches to specific questions that are offered by serious thinkers, I have a more modest project in mind—to explore how the Catholic social tradition might consider key questions about the justice of taxation.

Focusing on the Catholic social tradition, though, presents a third set of challenges. First, the tradition—notably the papal magisterium of the last 125 years or so—has had virtually nothing to say about taxation and fiscal policy. And what little the popes have said, as we will see, has tended to be anodyne and general. So, we have to interrogate the tradition, so to speak, to identify principles that can be applied to particular issues. Fortunately, there is some literature from various professional perspectives that attempts to do this—but this leads to a second specific challenge.

The Catholic social tradition, after all, is not unitary and it is not dogmatic. That is, there are different voices within the tradition that disagree, that attach different meanings to key concepts, that are shaped to one degree or another by conceptual frameworks alien to the Catholic tradition, and that arrive at different conclusions about particular moral questions (and the attendant moral obligations).

In spite of this variety, I remain convinced that there is an authentic Catholic social doctrine, deeply embedded in and deriving its conceptual framework from classical moral theology, in the spirit of Augustine, Aquinas, and others.[1] Our

1 I think it is fair to make a distinction between the social *doctrine* of the Church and the Catholic social *tradition*. The doctrine of the Church comprises concepts, principles, and preferences that the Church has endorsed in some formal way. Unlike some of

first task, then, is to achieve some clarity about foundational concepts, such as the nature of the person, the common good, justice, and ownership. We can then apply these concepts to questions about taxation, in conversation to some degree with other views but principally with the goal of clarifying how the Catholic social tradition might offer answers.

To this end, permit me to offer some general observations about the social tradition before we move to particular concepts.

The early Church had little confidence in the possibility of changing the ways of the world. Instead, the first Christians characteristically sought to change men and women in the world and turn them to God. Criticism of the ways of the earthly city was a natural consequence of Christian convictions that the world was corrupted by sin and that Jesus offered an avenue out of that corruption. Saint Augustine's development of the idea of two cities, a city of men (that we now inhabit) and a city of God (for which we are destined), was an extended exploration of the limits of Christian action in the world.[2]

the dogmatic statements in areas of theology like Christology or sacraments, nothing about the social doctrine of the Church has been taught irreformably. By contrast, the social tradition is a two-thousand-year-old conversation among Catholic clergy, theologians, and laity about all matters social. Though by and large inspired by the same faith, the participants in this conversation offer different and sometimes sharply conflicting views about social questions. One should avoid confusing the *tradition* with the much more limited body of *doctrine*.

2 Despite modern claims to the contrary, the early Christians were not social revolutionaries nor has the Church historically been an advocate of revolution. While this posture may sometimes reflect an unhealthy entanglement of the Church with secular powers, it derives more deeply from lived experience, which indicates that revolutions rarely leave populations in better circumstances than before. The American experience is a rare exception.

Later the Church gained confidence that the world could indeed be reshaped through the conversion of individuals but retained a lively sense of the pervasive influence of sin. From time to time, though, Christians have lapsed into a kind of quietism, or discouragement about their capacity to influence the culture, and it has been necessary to reawaken the Church to its social mission.

At the other extreme, many in the Church in recent decades have embraced a view that the world can not only be made much less corrupt but that it can and should be perfected, or at least that fundamental systemic problems can be solved (e.g., poverty can be eliminated, or education and medical care can be provided abundantly to everyone). This yields an impatience with less-than-perfect outcomes and a conviction that change must be systemic. Taken even further, it yields a conviction that "just" outcomes are the objective after all and that personal conversion is at best a means. (The history of the Catholic social tradition is partly a history of efforts to avoid the extremes of indifference and perfectionism.)

In light of this we should also remember that, as a practical matter, the Church's social doctrine tends to present *principles*, not *prescriptions*. That is to say, the Church generally does not endorse a specific form of government or a specific economic structure or a specific culture.[3] It can support and work with a variety of systems to the extent that they genuinely respect and protect human dignity. On the other hand, systems that begin from a radically defective understanding of the human person, such as communism, fascism, or radical individualism, are inimical to Catholic faith and cannot be endorsed.

---

3 "In virtue of her mission and nature, [the Church] is bound to no particular form of human culture, nor to any political, economic, or social system." Second Vatican Council, *Gaudium et spes* (1965), no. 42.

Furthermore, the social tradition of the Church, as the Second Vatican Council reminds us, is not the possession of any individual person and so no one (save perhaps the pope and the bishops) is empowered to say that the Church endorses or condemns any concrete system or practice.[4] Given the nature of the Church, of the tradition, and of human societies, we commonly see that there is (and should be) considerable agreement on moral principles while people committed to these principles may disagree profoundly on the prudential application—the specific policies and practices to be followed in concrete cases—of the principles.

The Coherence of the Tradition

A modern author has noted that it is not unreasonable for people to think that the Church's social doctrine is "a box of spare parts."[5] In fact, Catholic social doctrine is incompletely developed and not fully coherent (in the sense of being well ordered and derived from foundational principles). There are several reasons for this. One is that the subject matter of the doctrine is particularly complicated, given that it is concrete and therefore determined to some degree by the circumstances of time and place. Its details are often a matter of experience and prudence. It is a work in progress that, at best, can yield guidelines for practical judgment rather than absolute principles.[6]

---

4 Second Vatican Council, *Gaudium et spes* (1965), no. 43.

5 See Clodovis Boff, "The Social Teaching of the Church and the Theology of Liberation: Opposing Social Practices?" in *Christian Ethics: Uniformity, Universality, Pluralism*, Concilium, vol. 150, ed. Jacques Pohier and Dietmar Mieth (New York: Seabury, 1981), 17–22.

6 See *Compendium of the Social Doctrine of the Church* (Vatican City: Libreria Editrice Vaticana, 2004), no. 72.

Another reason for the doctrine's lack of coherence has to do with its relationship with secular social theories. There is an analogy to be made with the experience of the early Church. The biblical theology of the Fathers was limited in its articulation and development until it could effectively incorporate the more sophisticated concepts and language of Greek philosophy. But even there, the Church over time learned that some philosophical concepts were helpful, while others were antithetical to its theological convictions.

In a similar way, the Church's social doctrine, as a work in progress, still struggles to develop the technical concepts and language that will allow it to develop more fully. In the meantime, it has often embraced concepts and language from secular theories (e.g., Aristotelian political theory, Roman law, Marxist analysis, modern economic and social theories, and Progressive political theory) that are sometimes helpful and sometimes misleading. In some sense, the social doctrine is like a giant jigsaw puzzle: the pieces are on the table but so are many that do not belong to the puzzle, and the finished picture is hard to bring into focus.

Ironically, there is an argument to be made that many modern social theories are in fact derived (as distortions) from the not-fully-articulate Catholic social tradition. For example, socialism embraces the Catholic conviction about the equal dignity of all persons but distorts this into a commitment to the equality of condition of all persons.[7] Neoclassical economics embraces the Catholic conviction about the importance of freedom but

[7] Jacques Maritain, for example, insisted that Marxism was a Christian heresy of sorts. See Maritain, *The Person and the Common Good* (New York: Charles Scribner's Sons, 1947), 88, as well as his collection of essays, *The Peasant of the Garonne* (New York: Holt, Rinehart and Winston, 1968), 200.

distorts it to diminish the social nature of persons and to deny the notion of objective human goods.

The continuing challenge for Catholic social doctrine is to develop and bear witness to a comprehensive, consistent, and balanced vision of a good society. This is especially difficult in the face of urgent problems, made all the more pressing by modern media, and by the lure of so many tempting solutions. The difficulty is compounded by the fact that it is the laity, relatively unversed in theological categories, who are chiefly responsible for addressing these problems. The Church's contribution is to encourage the world not to forget the poor and vulnerable but also to provide some lenses through which we might evaluate the solutions on offer. It falls to the laity, then, to employ these lenses as they seek to craft effective responses to real problems.

Ultimately, the objective of this volume is to offer a view through these lenses of the way in which questions about taxation might be considered. If the Catholic tradition is rooted in a correct vision of the person and of the nature of genuine human fulfillment, then these lenses have something to offer to anyone concerned about justice and taxation.

II The Human Person and Human Flourishing

The most fundamental concept that we need to engage has to do with our understanding of the nature, the true situation, and the authentic flourishing of human persons. This topic, of course, plays an enormous role in questions of medical ethics but our concern here is not principally with protections for human dignity. Instead, our convictions about the human person will shape our views about what constitutes general human welfare, both for individuals and as a quality of a society. And since on most accounts, the state has some level of responsibility for promoting human welfare, the answers we give to this question inevitably affect tax policy.

Any discussion of the Catholic vision of the human person must begin with the conviction that human persons are images of God and in virtue of that reality they are endowed with a fundamental and irreducible value or dignity. No human person is without this basic dignity, no person strictly as such has greater value than another, and while this dignity can be violated, it cannot be extinguished. Persons may depend upon government for protection, and while they may be ignored or abused by government, their dignity does not derive from the state nor is it conferred by the general will or any other convention. On the Catholic view, human dignity is an objective reality, not a social construct.

As an image of God, an *imago Dei*, the human person is intelligent (that is, rational), free (capable of self-direction, choice, and initiative), and social. This last means that human persons, by nature and not merely by necessity, form and belong to communities of all sorts, from families to societies.[1] Indeed, outside a community, the development and fulfillment of a person as a human being is impossible. Human communities are not merely expedients but utterly essential for human flourishing.[2]

---

1 The relatively modern notion that human persons by nature are radical individuals, as proposed by Thomas Hobbes for example, stands in sharp opposition to the Catholic vision of the person. Hobbes and those who embrace this view sometimes imagine an original, pre-social state of nature in which persons live as isolated individuals but decide, for reasons of expediency, to form voluntary communities defined by a sort of social contract. A more reasonable account of human origins would reject such an artificial circumstance, at least by acknowledging that persons come to be in families, which are the original and inescapable social units. Hobbesian individualism has infected much Western thinking and generated unnecessary conflicts, both real and intellectual. For example, we might more productively understand the economy—and this has tax implications—not as an economy of individuals but as an economy of families. That is, the normal unit of economic analysis should be the family, not the individual. The family participates in the economy through work and consumption, the family owns and transfers wealth, the family is affected by unemployment, and so on.

2 Recognition of the essential social nature of human persons is the foundation for the claim that individuals have general rights to participate in communities and, more specifically, in cultural, economic, and political activities.

Indeed, the good of civic friendship, which we hope to achieve and sustain in a well-ordered society, is an essential component of human flourishing.

A bishop of the second century, St. Irenaeus of Lyons, commented that "the glory of God is man fully alive."[3] In biblical terms, "glory" is a manifestation of goodness. Irenaeus's comment suggests that one manifestation of the goodness of God is a flourishing human person, in whom the capacities to reason, to act, and to participate in community are fully realized. A more modern expression of the same idea is found in the notion of "integral human development." Pope Paul VI introduced this phrase into the papal literature and spoke of "the good of every man and of the whole man."[4] This "good" includes but is not limited to material goods; development does not simply mean the optimization of factors quantifiable in economic measures.[5] The development of a person or a community requires a foundation of material resources, since human persons are *embodied* spirits, but since we are embodied *spirits* the satisfaction of our material needs is never enough. Ultimately, on the Christian view, the development of the person is fulfilled in the transcendent

3 St. Irenaeus of Lyons, *Adversus haereses*, 4.20.5–7. See also the *Catechism of the Catholic Church*, nos. 293–94.

4 Pope Paul VI, *Populorum Progressio* (1967), nos. 14–15.

5 Welfare economics, as a sub-specialty in the field, sought to measure human well-being in a society in terms of expressed (or observed) preferences and then to calculate how best to distribute resources to achieve an optimum satisfaction of preferences throughout the community as a whole given the constraint of resource limitations. In fact, though, many of the nonmaterial aspects of human fulfillment are simply not quantifiable and inevitably a bias emerges toward supporting material factors.

destiny to which every person is called, which is an intimate share in the life of the God who made us.[6]

In this life, however, it is critical to note that human persons are agents, not merely passive consumers. Integral human development, therefore, aims at realizing in action the full capacity of persons to reason well, to act well, and to participate in community.[7] This requires certain immaterial resources and conditions, such as education, peace (the "tranquility of order," in St. Augustine's phrase), and freedom to act as one ought. And it requires personal initiative. Development, whether of a person or a community, is not something that one person (or community) can do to or for another. Development is a personal (or communal) duty, a response to a vocation, for which there is no substitute.[8] To be sure, others can provide resources and assistance, but to suppress or attempt to substitute for the free initiative of the person or the community is to impede development and to do a great injustice.[9]

---

6 Pope Leo XIII offers an emphatic reminder of this destiny in *Rerum Novarum*, no. 18.

7 Participation in community involves such things as forming friendships and families, working, and exchanging goods and services in the marketplace, as well as engaging in cultural, political, and religious activities.

8 On the Catholic view, persons and societies have a vocation, a call and invitation from the Creator, to contribute in concrete ways to the welfare of others, to the unfolding of creation, and to the building of the kingdom.

9 See Pope Paul VI, *Populorum Progressio*, nos. 14–15, 34; Pope St. John XXIII, *Mater et Magistra*, no. 51, Pope Benedict XVI, *Caritas in Veritate* (2009), nos. 16–17.

There may be formidable obstacles, however, to achieving these aspirations for individuals or for nations, some of which are matters of chance or fortune, while others are consequences of the human condition. Some of these obstacles can be overcome by hard work and ingenuity but others are not susceptible to the application of technology. There are factors internal to persons that must be addressed in other ways. In the West, classical moral philosophy from Plato and Aristotle forward has examined these factors and Christianity supplements this work. Revelation reveals man to himself and teaches us that the world in which we live has defects that were not intended by the Creator. These defects are the consequence of human sinfulness and cannot be eliminated as long as this sinfulness persists. To return to St. Augustine's powerful image, we inhabit the City of Men but are destined to live in the City of God.

The City of Men should be familiar to us. While it includes many good and beautiful elements, it is also characterized by injustice, selfishness, abuse of power and trust, and many other evils. On some views, these evils are structural in nature. If the right structures and the right policies could be set in place, the evils could be much diminished if not eliminated entirely. This might entail entirely overturning some systems through revolutionary action (as Marx thought) or less dramatically by repairing structures through political and civic action. For example, if tax policies could be reformed so that everyone paid his or her fair share, many problems could be resolved.

While acknowledging that many structures, policies, and practices in society are defective and dysfunctional, the Catholic tradition resists the notion that the fundamental remedy is simply structural change, whether by revolution or by well-intentioned expert design. Genuinely effective remedies depend upon personal conversion because the root cause of social ills is sin. Replacing structures that were designed and set in place by sinful people with new structures that are designed and set in place by other sinful people, is not a formula for lasting and significant reform. Treating symptoms may reduce the harms temporarily but unless the root causes are addressed new evils will arise.[10]

How, then, should the Christian live in the City of Men? The Christian vocation, especially the vocation of the laity in the City of Men, seems to have two dimensions. On one hand, the Church has always understood that it is called "to relieve the misery of the suffering" in immediate and concrete ways, even where that requires significant sacrifice on the part of the Church as a community and on the part of individual Christians. This is both a sign of the love of God and a mode of Christian discipleship.[11]

At the same time, the Church has a duty to witness to a deeper reality about human life: its redemption and orientation to a goal and a fulfillment beyond the scope of economics and politics. This orientation and the events in human history that follow from it constitute a different sort of progress, "radically transformed by the new outlook created by Christian faith, assuring us that progress is possible only because God the Father has decided from the beginning to make man a sharer of his glory in Jesus Christ.... In him God wished to conquer sin and make it serve our greater good, which infinitely surpasses what progress could achieve."[12] Here we are reminded that secular visions of progress, while not to be dismissed out of hand, may nevertheless seek to perfect social and political institutions that are inherently impermanent. Some danger lies

---

10 Pope St. John Paul II, *Sollicitudo Rei Socialis* (1987), nos. 35–38.

11 Pope St. John Paul II, *Sollicitudo Rei Socialis* (1987), nos. 30–31; Pope Benedict XVI, *Deus Caritas Est* (2005), no. 29.

12 Pope St. John Paul II, *Sollicitudo Rei Socialis* (1987), no. 31.

in choosing inappropriate means to pursue an elusive goal that mimics, and without grace cannot achieve, the ends offered by the divine plan.[13]

[13] Proponents of some tax policies seem to believe that basic and enduring social problems—poverty, provision of medical care for all, and others—can be resolved if only sufficient revenue can be raised through taxation. That these problems have not been resolved yet, in their view, is less an issue of resources than of political will. A more realistic, Augustinian view, echoed by some of the modern popes, is that these problems are more fundamentally a consequence of human sinfulness. The problems can be moderated by both individual and collective action but as long as sinfulness persists, they cannot be eliminated. See, for example, Pope Leo XIII, *Rerum Novarum* (1891), no. 14; and St. John Paul II, *Sollicitudo Rei Socialis* (1987), nos. 35–37.

III Common Goods

In the language of classical moral philosophy, anything that serves as the object of intentional human action is a *good* or at least an *apparent* good.[1] While some goods are private, meaning they can only be possessed or enjoyed by one person, a great many goods are held in common, meaning they can be possessed, used, enjoyed, or pursued by a number of people. When one first realizes that human persons are naturally social beings and that their genuine fulfillment inevitably involves a community of some sort, one begins to understand the critical importance of common goods. Attempts to understand and resolve issues of justice in a community must sooner or later deal with the question of what it means for goods to be common. Unfortunately, the term *common good* is one of the most equivocal in the field of social ethics. Equivocation on this term (and the frequent failure to identify explicitly the meaning intended in a particular context) is the cause of a great deal of intellectual mischief.

---

1 Aristotle famously observed that we all seek what we believe to be good. We may be mistaken about what is genuinely and objectively good but we never deliberately pursue some goal because we believe it to be evil. We are attracted to the good, even on occasions when we might be willing to tolerate some great evil in order to obtain what we desire.

It can be misleading to speak of *the* common good—as if there were only one good (or collection of goods) that could properly be called common. Thomas Aquinas reminds us that, in a fundamental way, human persons are ordered to three common goods. The first of these is a set of conditions in a society that, if perfect, would enable each and every member of the community to flourish. These conditions, which are never perfectly and fully constituted in the City of Man, are means to an end.[2] The second common good is an end in itself and a critical element of a good human life on the natural level. It is the active participation of individuals in the life of the community—what the tradition sometimes calls "civic friendship."[3] The third common good is also an end in itself, though a supernatural one. It is beatitude, the sharing in the life of God that is the transcendent destiny of all human persons.

The modern Catholic social tradition often refers to the instrumental common good of a society as *the* common good, though the Magisterium is quite clear that there are others.[4]

---

2 The good sought in any human action is either a *final* good (an end in itself), or an *instrumental* good (a means to another end). Speculative knowledge that is not immediately useful but satisfies curiosity is one kind of final good, as are most forms of play and aesthetic experience. Money, power, and academic degrees (as distinct from the knowledge gained by studying for the degree) are all instrumental goods.

3 The prominent twentieth-century Catholic philosopher, Jacques Maritain, spoke of civic friendship as "a profane [i.e., secular] image of brotherly love." See *Scholasticism and Politics* (New York: Macmillan, 1940), 109. Maritain had in mind the fraternal charity that would characterize the kingdom of heaven.

4 See, for example, Pope Leo XIII, *Rerum Novarum* (1891), no. 18, and Pope St. John XXIII, *Pacem in Terris* (1963), no. 38.

The formal definition generally used was first offered by Pope St. John XXIII in 1961: "[The common good] embraces the sum total of those conditions of social living whereby men are enabled more fully and more readily to achieve their own perfection."[5]

Totalitarian states make the serious mistake of regarding such instrumental common goods as absolutely final and so in the end become willing to sacrifice all manner of private goods for their sake. Even in wiser societies, caution must always be exercised in crafting and applying positive laws so that the conditions that must exist in a society to promote the flourishing of its members are adequately protected while at the same time private goods are not threatened. To be sure, in any society, some private goods are incompatible with sustaining these public conditions and so may be legitimately curtailed—but a prudent balance must nevertheless be maintained.

One further note: We should remember that different conceptions of the common good are in use by different philosophical or political groups. Utilitarians, for example, may consider the common good to be the greatest good for the greatest number, which implies that the good of some innocent persons might reasonably be sacrificed so that others may benefit. Libertarians are inclined to deny that human persons have common ends and to think of the common good as a set of conditions that provides maximal freedom to individuals to pursue their idiosyncratic and voluntaristic goals. Progressives, for their part, may see the common good, not as a set of conditions, but as the actual achievement of a desired distribution of material and immaterial

[5] Pope St. John XXIII, *Mater et Magistra* (1961), no. 65. This definition was repeated in John's later encyclical, *Pacem in Terris* (1963), no. 58, and by the Second Vatican Council, *Gaudium et Spes* (1965), no. 26, as well as by the *Compendium of the Social Doctrine of the Church* (2004), no. 164.

resources among members of a community. And we should also remember that, while the instrumental common good as the Church understands it is never fully or perfectly developed, it is still a reasonable ambition for all Christians to defend it as needed and to improve it as possible.

IV Justice, Authority, and Law

We use the word so often that one might suppose we all agree on the meaning of *justice*. But in truth, questions about the nature of justice, about what is just or unjust in concrete circumstances, and about remedies that ought to be applied where injustice is claimed are never easy to resolve to everyone's satisfaction. The history of Western philosophy is full of countless investigations into justice, from Plato's *Republic* and Aristotle's *Nicomachean Ethics* through Aquinas, Hume, Kant, Bentham, and Rawls to books and articles published today. As Alasdair MacIntyre has clearly revealed and as is well known to philosophers, there are many rival theories of justice, which tend to be hidden in the background of our public discussions but nevertheless ensure that we will not reach consensus.[1]

Still, philosophers (and more recently lawyers, theologians, economists, political scientists, and journalists) attempt to defend their preferred theory of justice and to dismiss its rivals as defective, somewhat irrational, and even incorrigibly biased. Perhaps readers will forgive me (and probably thank me) for not attempting to survey this arena and drag them into its

---

1 Alasdair MacIntyre, *Whose Justice? Which Rationality?* (South Bend: University of Notre Dame Press, 1988).

conflicts.[2] Having said that, I do not despair of seeking and achieving a significant measure of clarity about justice in the world at large or in the field of taxation. I am persuaded that the classical tradition of moral philosophy, most prominently represented by Aristotle and Aquinas, and largely embraced by Catholic moral theology (as well as the deeper traditions of Anglo-American law), is in fact a robust and reliable tool for understanding and securing justice in society. While it may be appropriate to allude to other theories of justice from time to time, my principal intention in this volume is to explore what the Catholic social tradition can contribute to our understanding of the ethics (i.e., justice) of taxation.

Whether openly acknowledged or not, the starting point for any serious consideration of the nature of justice is a set of convictions about the nature of the person and the constitution of human flourishing. However it is understood, justice always concerns other people; no one can be meaningfully just or unjust to himself. For a hermit (setting aside his relationship with God) there are never issues of justice. Furthermore, questions of justice always begin with a *debitum*, or an obligation. What is owed to the other? We cannot answer that in any depth unless we understand what it means to be a person and what persons require.

The Catholic moral tradition on justice is, in some sense, the result of an encounter between biblical faith and Greek philosophy (especially the work of Plato and Aristotle). Biblical faith, the response to God's revelation in history, contributes a vision of human persons—of their dignity and destiny—that goes beyond the insights of Greek philosophy. For its part,

---

2 MacIntyre laments that discussions about justice, among philosophers as well as others, tend not to be searches for what is true but instead occasions to marshal clever arguments in order to defeat one's opponents on a rhetorical battlefield. See *Whose Justice?*, 5.

Greek philosophy provides a conceptual framework, a vocabulary, and a set of rigorous analytical tools that can tease out the implications of biblical faith in great depth. What emerged from this encounter was not a distortion of either tradition but a new synthesis, refined over many centuries into a distinctive moral tradition that has shaped the Church's pastoral work and canonical system.[3]

The Catholic moral tradition begins with the individual person as a free agent. Justice is first of all understood to be a virtue, a stable characteristic, of persons.[4] (In the most confusing and difficult practical situations, the real measure of justice is not an impersonal calculation but rather what the judgment of a truly just person would dictate be done.) By extension, the adjective *just* can be applied not only to persons but also to actions and to rules.[5] The classic formal definition of a just person, which has

3 See Pope Benedict XVI, "Faith, Reason, and the University: Memories and Reflections" (A lecture given at the University of Regensburg, 12 September 2006). Available at http://w2.vatican.va/content/benedict-xvi/en/speeches/2006/september/documents/hf_ben-xvi_spe_20060912_university-regensburg.html. As Pope Benedict observed, there were movements in the twentieth century that sought to disentangle Christian theology from its Greek framework and to recover a purer, more authentic Christian morality. While it is true that some expositions of moral theology, especially in the nineteenth and early twentieth centuries, emphasized the technical to the neglect of the personal, the remedy was not to dismiss philosophy. Today there are signs of the opposite trend, with some theologians arguing that a biblical morality can be discerned and ought to be embraced over and against the analytic character of the classical tradition. Benedict would not agree, though he would endorse the importance of balance.

4 Aquinas frequently says that a virtue is a characteristic that makes a person's acts good and makes that person good as well.

5 In a secondary sense, it may also be applied, and often is applied, to outcomes. But just or unjust outcomes, properly speaking, are

been peacefully accepted by the Catholic tradition for most of its history, was offered by Ulpian, an influential third-century Roman jurist and scholar. He said that a just person is one who, "by a constant and perpetual will renders to each person what is his due."[6] That is, a just person is one who always and everywhere, as a fixed element of his character, is committed to giving to others what they deserve, or have a right to receive. Consequently, a just act is one that actually gives to another what that person deserves to have, and a just rule is an ordering principle that specifies just acts.[7]

This account of justice also implies something prior. That is, if justice requires us to give to others what they are due, there must be some prior reason to account for *what* they are due. For that we must look to something more fundamental than justice and, not surprisingly, that will take us back to our understanding of the human person.

One of the most fundamental yearnings of the human spirit is for order. The story of the fall in the third chapter of Genesis can be understood as a rejection by Adam of the order established by the Creator and a desire for himself to be the source of order in his world. ("You will be like God, knowing good and evil" Gen. 3:5, NRSVCE). The consequence of Adam's sin, of course, is that he received what he wanted, he was "freed" to establish an order of his own without God's guidance and power.

---

the results of just or unjust actions or rules. As will be evident later, unequal outcomes are often the result of chance and, while unfortunate and regrettable, such outcomes are neither just nor unjust.

6 Quoted, for example, by St. Thomas Aquinas, *Summa Theologiae*, II-II, Q. 58, art. 1.

7 It may be noted that someone who is not habitually a just person may still perform a just act or even originate and enforce a just rule. Such a person, though, cannot be expected to do so consistently nor would others be wise to rely on his judgment about the justice of particular situations.

He still sought order, of course, but it was elusive, his power and intelligence no longer adequate to the challenges he faced.

The struggle to establish and sustain order in life against the factors of disorder is the story of human culture. On the Judeo-Christian account, human sinfulness, beginning with Adam, is the principal source of chaos in our world. Instinctively we grasp that things were not meant to be this way, that order is deeper than chaos and necessary for human flourishing.

Order, however, implies an end or a goal. A complex system is well-ordered if the parts function together in service of the goal. An individual human life is well-ordered if a person's choices and actions are consistent with and mutually supportive of integral human development and genuine flourishing. Chaos is introduced if the parts of a system, or of a life, are ordered to mutually exclusive and conflicting goals.

Something similar is true of human communities, whether families, associations, or societies. A community is well-ordered if the actions of its members support and do not undermine the goals of the community that in one way or another serve some aspects of human flourishing. Multiple goals can be pursued if they are not in conflict with one another. This might be the case, for example, in a business with two distinct operating divisions that both contribute to the overall success of the business but do not compete with one another for resources or customers. Very often, well-ordered communities pursue multiple goals that are nested, that is, where some goals are more immediate or subordinate to others but nevertheless complementary. In the Catholic tradition, this is the case for a society as a whole, where a variety of ends may be pursued that are ordered, first, to the natural development and flourishing of its members as individuals; second, to their participation in the life of the community; and third, to their supernatural destiny.[8]

On the natural level, we are subject to a two-dimensional order with respect to our fulfillment as persons. One dimension is the realization of our potential as *individuals*—the development of our personal capacities to reason well, to choose well, and to act well. The instrumental common good of a society is the entire set of conditions that makes this development possible. The second order is the realization of our potential as *social* beings—our actual participation in communities, enjoyment of friendships, engagement with culture, collaboration with others in the pursuit of common goals, and so forth. This is a substantive common good, and it fulfills an essential element of our humanity.[9]

We might say that justice is the order, the harmony, and the equality that ought to exist between persons, whether as individuals in a casual relationship or as members of a community. Starting with the person as the subject of just acts (that is, as the agent, the one who acts), we can begin to distinguish several kinds of justice. These distinctions are often misunderstood, but they will be critical for our discussion of issues in taxation.

The tradition distinguishes between *particular* justice and *general* justice (or we might say, justice in general). Particular justice recognizes two possible ways in which an acting indi-

---

8 While our concern here is with the natural development of persons, we should note that this level of development is in some sense also ordered to our transcendent destiny.

9 A third order, of course, is the common good of beatitude, a supernatural destiny of persons. A proper ordering of a natural society, while a good in itself, is not the cause of our supernatural destiny. Nevertheless, a proper order entails eliminating obstacles to holiness.

vidual can be related to others, either as a private person or as a person in authority.

Particular Justice

Acting as a private person is by far the more common and describes most of our interactions with others. The justice of private persons who are equal in fundamental dignity to all other private persons is named *commutative*[10] or *corrective* by the tradition. This happens in countless ways. When we purchase something in a store, we receive something of value and our payment restores the equality of buyer and seller. When we receive a compliment or a gift, an expression of gratitude restores harmony. If we harm other persons or damage their property, we are obligated in justice to restitution, which once again restores the equality between us.[11] The key to understanding commutative justice, then, is that it aims at the restoration of a simple equality between parties. Once this form of justice is established, neither party is in debt to the other. (The tradition often speaks of this as an "arithmetic" equality.) The personal status or situation of the parties is irrelevant to sustaining equality.[12]

---

[10] From the Latin word *commutatio*, this means "change," or "exchange." The implication is that commutative justice comes into play when some change has taken place between persons.

[11] Of course, in some cases the harm we do cannot adequately be corrected. (Think of many crimes against persons.) Aside from making what restitution we can, apology and forgiveness seek to restore harmony and equality. In some sense, to forgive is to release the other party from the debt incurred.

[12] This irrelevance can be misunderstood, so permit me a couple of quick examples. If I buy a loaf of bread, the just price should be the same whether I am hungry or not. If I purchase medicine for a sick child, the pharmacist should not increase the price because

On the other hand, an individual may act in authority, distributing benefits and burdens on behalf of the community as a whole. (It is important to note that the benefits and burdens distributed are in some sense the property of the community, not the property of individual members.) For example, suppose a community has a supply of a vaccine available to prevent a certain disease. If the quantity of the vaccine is more than enough to give everyone an adequate dose, the issue of justice in distribution is fairly simple: everyone gets an adequate dose and there is no need to ration the vaccine. However, if the quantity is limited and insufficient to give everyone a dose, then a person in authority must determine how it is to be justly distributed. Where commutative justice takes no account of the personal status or situation of the parties involved, distributive justice must do so.

The general rule for distributive justice is that persons who are alike in relevant ways must be treated alike, but persons who are different in relevant ways may be treated differently. In this case, a civil authority might justly distribute the vaccine first to persons who are most likely to contract the disease or likely to suffer the most serious consequences. That is, the vaccine might first be given to medical personnel (who are most exposed to the disease), or to the elderly, or to children. No injustice is done if persons least likely to contract the disease, or most likely to resist its worst effects, are last to be vaccinated. But an injustice is done if irrelevant factors are used to determine the distribution—for

he notices how worried I am. In each instance, my personal situation is irrelevant, and it would be unjust for the seller to change the price to take advantage of my distress. On the other hand, the baker or the pharmacist might acknowledge my situation and instead of entering into a sales transaction, make me a gift of the bread or medicine. In this case, it is a different interaction, but I now have an obligation of gratitude, which restores our equality.

instance, if persons are vaccinated on account of their personal relationship with the civil authority or because of their celebrity or in return for favors offered. Something quite similar is true of the distribution of burdens, such as jury duty, or military service, or taxes. In every instance, where commutative justice seeks a simple (or arithmetic) equality between persons, distributive justice properly seeks a proportional (or geometric) equality.[13]

While the subject of distributive justice is principally the civil authority who acts in specific cases, the private persons who are affected by the final decision participate, so to speak, in distributive justice by peacefully accepting the decision. Think of it as just reciprocity of a sort.

It is also worth remarking that distributive justice always concerns the distribution of something "belonging" to the community. This might be a supply of vaccine or the deployment of a fire department or public honors or the share of a tax burden. It never concerns the (re)distribution of privately owned property to pursue some public objective. It is not a matter of distributive justice, properly speaking, to confiscate income or wealth from some private persons in order to give it to other private persons in pursuit of a more equitable distribution of the national wealth.[14]

---

13 In our example, this would be true even with a sufficient supply of vaccine. Doses usually vary according to body size, so an adult would receive more of the vaccine than a small child, though in each case the dose would be proportionately the same.

14 Terms such as *the wealth of the nation* or *the national income* can be misleading. Strictly speaking they refer to an aggregate measure of the total wealth possessed or income received by (mostly) private persons over a defined period of time, not to the wealth or income possessed by the nation (i.e., the state). Consequently, neither the wealth of the nation nor the national income is a sum possessed by the community and available for distribution at the discretion of civil authority. That said, the distribution of private wealth and

General Justice

So much for particular justice, in which the objects of justice are always private persons. We must also briefly consider *general* justice, in which the objects are the common goods, or the principal goods held in common, of a society. Another way of thinking about this is to note that in matters of particular justice the persons who are the objects of justice can be identified.[15] By contrast, the objects of general justice are not private persons but communities taken as wholes. Individuals have the duty to sustain and defend the principal goods held in common by these communities that, in turn, serve the well-being of their members. Again we begin with the subject of general justice—the acting person—and again we can identify two dimensions.

The first dimension has as its subject the person in the role of civil authority. We might think of this as a complement to distributive justice, where the objects are private persons as members of a community and the civil authority has a duty to distribute benefits and burdens justly. On the level of general justice, the duty of the person in authority is to frame concrete laws, regulations, policies, and practices that support the

---

income is never equal. Some persons always have more, sometimes very much more, than others. If some portion of the pattern of distribution is the result of fraud or corruption, it is entirely appropriate for civil authorities to take action to remedy the problem. But the remedy they employ is a matter of *commutative* justice because it aims to correct the injustices that led to the skewed distribution. As far as the Catholic tradition is concerned, in no instance is the confiscation of justly acquired private property for the purpose of redistribution a matter of *distributive* justice.

15 That is, in principle, we could enumerate and name each of the persons touched by particular justice. This might be the owner of the bakery, whom you pay for the loaf of bread, or it might be every purchaser of a product found defective and entitled to a refund.

instrumental common good of the community and facilitate the substantive common good, civic friendship. Since this dimension of justice is concerned most fundamentally with law and legislation, the tradition has usually named it *legal* justice. The person in authority here has a solemn duty to frame laws and regulations that truly serve the common goods and fully accord with the natural law. For their part, the private persons who are members of the society have a reciprocal duty, in legal justice, to obey sound laws and to respect persons in authority.

The second, broader dimension of general justice binds all members of a community, both private persons and civil authorities, and has as its object the common goods of the society. Unfortunately, the common vocabulary of the tradition also names this *general* justice. It may be easiest to think of this as a virtue, which would be a firm and stable inclination to serve the common goods of the society. More specifically, it would be an alertness to the common goods, a willingness to act on opportunities to serve them, and a firm commitment of will to avoid actions that would harm them.[16]

This idea of general justice comes closest to being a description of the foundational form of justice. Because, as social beings, our flourishing is necessarily connected to the common goods of the society in which we live, it is entirely rational that we be committed to act in support of them whenever possible and

16 This is precisely what Pope St. John Paul II described as the virtue of "solidarity," perhaps giving us a new name for general justice. He defined it as "a firm and persevering determination to commit oneself to the common good; that is to say to the good of all and of each individual, because we are all really responsible for all." This definition embraces both the instrumental common good of society, which serves the good of each individual, and civic friendship, which entails our concern for one another. See *Sollicitudo Rei Socialis* (1987), no. 38.

never against them.[17] However, this dimension of general justice does not specify how we must act concretely to support the common goods. Multiple possible courses of action are often present and the good order of society (itself a component of the instrumental common good) would inevitably be threatened if a great many people made well-intentioned but idiosyncratic choices.[18] For this reason, general justice requires legal justice, which specifies what courses of action are obligatory for that society on contingent matters. For example, general justice, I submit, would incline persons to provide financial support to government so that it can perform its legitimate operations. But without the rules that arise from the exercise of legal justice, virtually no one would be in a position to know what would constitute just financial support in a given society at a given time. The abstract obligation, so to speak, would be actualized by laws and regulations concerning taxation.

---

17 A small point, perhaps, but many of our actions on a day-to-day basis have little impact on the common goods of society. The reference here to "opportunities" is not meant to suggest that just persons only support the common goods when it is not inconvenient to do so, but rather that many of our choices do not entail an effect on these common goods. But lest we overlook the common goods, as we may be inclined to do in many cases, the virtuous person maintains an alertness to occasions where the common goods are involved.

18 Think about the chaos that would result if we each crafted our own sets of traffic rules, each set reasonable to a degree but each set different in critical ways. Building codes, as an example, not only aim to ensure public safety but also to eliminate much of the waste and confusion that would result if architects, engineers, and builders each followed their own set of standards and measurements.

The Role of Authority

So far, in our discussion, we have often mentioned civil authorities. A modern preoccupation, especially in the context of democracies, has been with the question of what grounds the right to exercise authority in a community. One common modern answer, which has some implications for how the Catholic tradition might consider questions of taxation, is that the legislator or executive has authority to act by delegation from the people of the community. That is, the legislator is not sovereign and has only that authority delegated from the people to be exercised according to their will. This has the implication that a legislator who does not discharge his office as the people wish him to do, who does not make the laws the people prefer him to make, may rightly be removed in favor of a more obliging legislator. What can be lost in this understanding is that the legislator would have a duty to serve the common good, regardless of the current biases of the community and that his rightful tenure in office depends on this, not the passions of the electorate.

Another answer, more common in an earlier era, is that the legislator (usually a king or emperor, though other names are used) is indeed sovereign and not subject to the approval of the community who nevertheless have a duty to obey. Such a legislator may make laws as he wills and may perhaps be above the law himself. The source of this person's authority may be some claim to divine appointment or preference, to some tradition of the community, or to nothing more than raw power. More thoughtful theorists suggest that members of the community implicitly surrender some portion of their autonomy in return for the benefits of law and that this surrender grounds the legitimacy of the legislator.

Classic thinkers in the Catholic social tradition offered a different answer. Their view was more nuanced and sophisticated than the others I have described. (In fact, a case can be made that these other views are distortions of the Catholic view.)

The classical view began with the conviction that human beings are social by nature—not isolated individuals as Hobbes and Locke would have it. As a consequence, communities of all sorts, but particularly families and societies, are inevitable and necessary for human well-being. But every community requires order; without it individual self-interest leads to dissolution, and goals that require collaboration cannot be achieved. This is especially true in a society, and it is especially necessary for a society to be ordered by authority.

Following St. Paul in his letter to the Romans, the Church has always understood the ultimate source of authority to be God, who exercises authority over and for the whole of creation.[19] Human persons who exercise authority, especially civil authorities who govern societies, are understood to share in God's authority by a sort of delegation. They are entrusted with care for the community and, therefore, are stewards of a sort.

Pope Leo XIII laid out this view in some detail in his encyclical *Diuturnum*, published in 1881. His intention was to defend the authority of the legislator but also to place it in context. This authority, he wrote, comes not from the people but from God who alone is sovereign: "No man has in himself or of himself the power of constraining the free will of others by fetters of authority.... This power resides solely in God, the Creator and Legislator of all things."[20] Citizens may choose who is to exercise this authority but they themselves are not the source of it. Furthermore, those who exercise authority in civil society, as

---

[19] See Romans 13:1–7.

[20] Pope Leo XIII, *Diuturnum* (1881), no. 11.

delegates of divine authority, so to speak, are strictly accountable to God for their service:

> But in order that justice may be retained in government it is of the highest importance that those who rule States should understand that political power was not created for the advantage of any private individual; and that the administration of the State must be carried on to the profit of those who have been committed to their care, not to the profit of those to whom it has been committed.... On this account they are warned in the oracles of the sacred Scriptures, that they will have themselves some day to render an account to the King of kings and Lord of lords; if they shall fail in their duty, that it will not be possible for them in any way to escape the severity of God.[21]

On this view, and in stark contrast with modern legal positivists, legislators, whether kings or parliaments, do not *make* laws.[22] They lack the sovereign authority to do so. Instead, on behalf of the common good, when they legislate, they affirm principles of the natural law (such as prohibitions against murder and theft, which are wrong regardless of whether the civil law expressly prohibits them) or they determine specifications of natural-law principles and of justice in particular circumstances. (Laws concerning taxation fall into this second category.)

Summary

In the Catholic tradition, we can understand justice and the kinds of justice by beginning with the person who acts. Justice and injustice are always the results of deliberate human choice.

---

21 Pope Leo XIII, *Diuturnum* (1881), no. 16. For a further, more recent explanation of many of these same points, see Pope St. John XXIII, *Pacem in Terris* (1963), nos. 46–54.

22 See Pope Leo XIII, *Immortale Dei* (1885), no. 18.

The person who acts is a subject who must be just and must act justly. Other persons are always the objects of the choices and actions of the one who acts. When these other persons are specific, identifiable individuals or identifiable members of a group, we speak about *particular* justice. When a just act seeks to restore or maintain a sort of absolute equality between persons, it is an instance of *commutative* justice. When it involves the sharing of benefits or burdens belonging to a community and the act seeks to sustain a proportional equality between persons, it is an instance of *distributive* justice.

On the other hand, when the objects of acts are not identifiable individuals but communities as a whole, we are speaking about *general* (we might even say "universal") justice. In one instance, the person acting must respect, or at least avoid harm to, the common good of the community in his private actions. This is sometimes also called *general* justice. In the second instance, the person acting is in some way a public authority who has a duty to make laws, regulations, and policies for the society. This person is obligated above all to serve the common good in doing this and so is engaged in acts of *legal* justice. In a secondary way, private persons have a duty in legal justice to obey just laws. According to the tradition, a just law must satisfy four criteria: (1) it must be reasonable, (2) it must be ordered to the common good, (3) it must be made by a proper authority, and (4) it must be made public.[23]

The nature of human persons requires that we live in communities and in societies that in turn cannot persist or function properly without authority. The ultimate source of authority is the author of creation and all legitimate human authorities participate, in some sense, in God's authority. Their duty is to serve the well-being of the members of society, particularly by sustaining, defending, and perfecting (as far as possible) the common goods.

---

23 See Thomas Aquinas, *Summa Theologiae*, I-II, Q. 90, art 4.

V The Good Society, the State, and the Church

To say that we are social animals is to say that it is our nature to associate with others in what we do. We do not form families, villages, clubs, companies, and societies simply because we find them to be useful tools in our pursuit of private goals. To be sure, they can be useful to us but participating in friendships and communities of all sorts is also an important part of our development and fulfillment as human beings. Participation in a community, indeed in a variety of communities, is thus a good in itself (and by the same token, a grave evil results when individuals are denied opportunities to participate).

On the Catholic view, human life is made possible and enriched by this variety of associations and communities, beginning with the family. The largest of these is known by different names: the nation, the political community, the society. It is less well-defined than most human communities, as its boundaries are loosely marked and fluid. It contains within itself most other communities (not including the Church), but it does not contain them simply as parts. Other communities, such as families, are not parts of society in the way that, say, the heart or the lungs are parts of an animal. Many other communities are wholes in themselves, which is to say that their reason for being is not merely to serve the society. They flourish in a well-ordered society and contribute to that larger whole, but they also serve objectives of their own—genuine human goods—independently of what they offer to society.

There is a balance to be maintained in any good society. Individuals only develop as human persons within a healthy society; they cannot hold society at arm's length and treat it merely as a tool and expect to be fully human. At the same time, the society cannot absorb individuals by governing every aspect of their lives or sacrificing them in service of the good of the whole (however that might be defined).

In the modern era, two broad tendencies in secular political thinking have challenged the Catholic vision of society, both of which have implications for tax policy and justice in taxation. One, classical liberalism (and its libertarian variant), has emphasized the primacy of the individual and the freedom of that individual to pursue whatever life goals he or she defines. Society is seen principally as an instrument to advance the individual. A good society is one that creates the conditions for individuals to serve one another through mutually beneficial exchanges. In some versions of this view, society can demand no more than that individuals respect the same liberty in others that they wish for themselves (by obeying reasonable laws) and that they compensate the state (as an organ of society) for any benefits they receive. The relationship between citizen and state, then, becomes basically that of a series of exchanges.

From the Catholic point of view, liberalism has several defects. One is that it undervalues the importance of community and participation as an end in itself. Another is that classical liberal and libertarian theories tend to exaggerate rights of private ownership and underemphasize the morally binding (if not legally enforceable) duties accompanying ownership. A third weakness is the tendency to diminish empathy and charity for those in need. In the end, in the liberal view, the good of a society is simply an aggregate of the good, or of the welfare of the individuals composing it.

The second alternative is one version or another of collectivism, which tends to regard the individual not as a whole in himself but merely as a part of the social whole. In its sterner manifestations, the good of society (or of the state) is conceived to be something above and independent of the well-being and flourishing of individuals. Where liberalism emphasizes the freedom and independence of the individual, collectivism denies independence and suppresses freedom in favor of the good of society. The relation of the individual to society tends to become that of part to whole, or servant to master. What is necessary for life comes from the state but only to those who serve it well. The order of the day is a rough sort of equality in subordination to the community and the state. Not surprisingly, collectivist societies have a strong tendency toward totalitarianism, in which the state ceases to be merely an organ of society and becomes instead identified with the social whole, extinguishing other associations and lower-order communities.[1] Nor is it surprising that they reject the legitimacy of many categories of private ownership, even claiming a Christian inspiration for this position. Thus, in a collectivist spirit the wealth of the

---

1 It is worthwhile to distinguish a *totalitarian* society from a *dictatorship*. In the model of a totalitarian society, virtually all human activities and relationships are governed by, or at least are subject to, the authority of the state. As Benito Mussolini said to the Italian Chamber of Deputies in 1927: "Everything in the State, nothing outside the State, nothing against the State." While totalitarian societies tend to become dictatorial (in which a person, or a committee, becomes the lawgiver and unaccountable source of authority in the society), this need not be the case. Christopher Dawson, the prominent twentieth-century Catholic historian, was concerned that modern democratic societies were strongly inclined to be totalitarian, though not dictatorial (in the worst sense). See "What Is a Christian Civilization?" in *The Historic Reality of Christian Culture* (Routledge & Kegan Paul, 1960), 40.

society, which on the liberal view is an aggregate measure of the wealth of individual members of society, can become the wealth belonging to the state (even if the state permits it to be in the temporary possession of individuals).[2]

In many respects, the Church's opposition to collectivism has been more aggressive than its criticism of liberalism, though it has consistently warned against the excesses of both movements. Each movement, in its own way, fails to honor the full truth about human persons. Liberalism is correct to recognize the freedom, independence, and rights to ownership of individuals but it exaggerates these features while it diminishes the importance of community, gratuity, and solidarity. Collectivism aspires to recognize the equal dignity of individuals and to emphasize duties to the community, but it fails to honor freedom and rights to ownership, often ending by denying many other human rights as well.

The Catholic conception of the good society stands as an alternative to both liberal/libertarian and collectivist visions. At its root are the convictions that societies are natural communities (not Hobbesian concessions to human sinfulness) and that a society and the culture that shapes it are larger than the state that governs it. To make this last point more concretely, there are a great many activities in a society that, unless they threaten public order, should not be managed by civil authorities. Indeed, rather than the state shaping culture, the culture that defines a people should naturally determine the shape of the state.

Furthermore, we can recognize three elements of a good society, each of which has implications for tax policy. According to

---

2 Note that in a thoroughly socialist society most forms of taxation are impossible. Taxation implies a certain amount of private property that can potentially be attached by the state. In a socialist society, where private property is virtually nonexistent, there is nothing for the state to attach; it already possesses the wealth of the nation.

the Catholic view, a good society is informed by the truth about human persons, is organic in structure, and is ordered by law.

First, no social arrangement can truly be good or successful if it is seriously mistaken about human nature and the goods that fulfill human persons.[3] Collectivist arrangements fail to recognize that the individual is not merely a part—and a dispensable part at that—of a larger social whole but is in fact whole in itself, with a dignity of his own, thriving within the whole that is society.[4] Liberal arrangements emphasize the freedom of the individual but fail to acknowledge what that freedom is for.[5] Both tend to exaggerate the economic element of social life to the diminishment of a more expansive and coherent view of the person.[6] As a consequence, both will fail, sooner or later and in different ways, to be the sort of community in which human persons can truly flourish.

The second element, the organic structure of society, conceives of the civil community as a composition of a rich variety of private associations, from the family to clubs and social organizations, businesses, universities, charitable associations, and so on. Many of these, especially the family, have particular and irreplaceable functions to perform within and for a society.

---

3 See Pope St. John Paul II, *Centesimus Annus* (1991), nos. 11, 13, 29.

4 On this point, see Jacques Maritain, *The Person and the Common Good* (New York: Charles Scribner's Sons, 1947), 37–48.

> Let us keep in mind this essential point … that, if the person of itself requires "to be part of" society, or "to be a member of society," this in no wise means that it must be in society in the way in which a part is in a whole and treated in society as a part in a whole. On the contrary, the person, as person, requires to be treated as a whole in society. (48)

5 Pope St. John Paul II, *Centesimus Annus* (1991), no. 25.

6 Pope St. John Paul II, *Centesimus Annus* (1991), nos. 19, 24.

Totalitarian societies of all shapes tend to suppress private associations, or they seek to absorb them within the state, with the result that nothing stands between the individual and the state. In contrast, the Church insists that a healthy society honors the principle of subsidiarity, which requires authorities to respect the proper function and relative independence of these associations and to help them achieve their ends where that help is necessary.[7] One of the implications of this element for our topic is that the state should moderate its involvement and, consequently, its demand for tax revenues, so as to create and protect space for the operation of private associations. Not all social-welfare activities, for example, properly belong to the state.[8] The Church is certainly committed to the idea of limited government, but the principle is that government should have the proper size and scope necessary to secure the common good of the society, not that it should be as small as possible.

The third element, the ordering of society under law, is the proper function of the state, for which there is no effective substitute in a good society. Civil authorities are responsible, as far as may be possible, for securing justice in society as a necessary condition of true civil peace. In whatever way is chosen by the community, they make, enforce, and are themselves bound by just laws, policies, and regulations. The state operates courts and otherwise provides for the broad infrastructure (transportation, communication, currency, defense of the nation, and so on)

---

7 See Pope Leo XIII, *Rerum Novarum* (1891), no. 28, where Leo insists that "the State must not absorb the individual or the family." This idea is made more explicit in Pope Pius XI, *Quadragesimo Anno* (1931), nos. 79–80, where Pius introduces the term *subsidiarity*. A good recent treatment of the concept, with an application to business, is Michael J. Naughton et al., *Respect in Action: Applying Subsidiarity to Business* (St. Paul: University of St. Thomas, 2015).

8 Pope Benedict XVI, *Deus Caritas Est* (2005), nos. 28–29.

required for the members of the society to carry on their lives and activities. For this the state justly demands the revenue it needs to function, but questions remain to be resolved about which functions civil authorities ought to engage and which they ought to leave to private parties. Citizens are generally free to assign a greater or lesser number of functions to the state, and at times civil authorities simply assume a range of functions. In any event, decisions about this have an immediate effect on the need for revenue and choices about tax structures. We will return to this topic but for now we note that in a good society a decision is first made about which functions a state is to perform, and then appropriate revenues are secured. The state should not consider the revenue it can obtain and then decide what new functions it can perform.

VI Ownership

It is commonplace to speak about property rights, but this is a misleading expression. What individuals and groups have is a right of ownership, and property is the object of this right; it is what is owned. Ownership and property have a correlative relationship (like parent and child). There is no ownership unless something is possessed as property; and an object cannot be called property unless someone owns it.

The Catholic social tradition has adopted what one might call a middle position on the legitimacy of private ownership of property. The very early Christian community in Jerusalem apparently held most property in common (see Acts 2:44–45), which has been the model more or less followed by most monastic communities and religious orders to the present day. In the later Middle Ages, some Christians moved beyond the notion of common ownership to insist aggressively that Christ and the apostles owned no property and that true Christians must also reject private ownership. Early in the fourteenth century, while acknowledging the value of freely chosen evangelical poverty (by professed religious, for example), the Church decisively repudiated the idea that private ownership of property is immoral or inconsistent with living a Christian life.

At the other extreme, Roman law, which was a source of inspiration for a good deal of canon law, was robust in its protection of the rights attached to private ownership, tending toward absolutism in this regard. By contrast, the Catholic social tradition affirmed the legitimacy of private ownership but at the same time insisted that the right to own property privately was qualified by other obligations. This question acquired a new urgency in the nineteenth century with the emergence of socialist movements in Europe, some of which insisted that private ownership of property was contrary to the good of society and must be extinguished.

The magisterial discussion of this question by the Church in modern times began with Pope Leo XIII's encyclical *Rerum Novarum* in 1891 and has continued through the publication in 2004 of the first official general summary of Catholic social doctrine, the *Compendium of the Social Doctrine of the Church.*

The Gift of Creation

In the Catholic view, the fundamental conviction concerning property is that the whole of earthly creation is a gift of the Creator to the human community, those living now and those yet to live, to support the well-being and flourishing of each and every person. The Church speaks of this as the *principle of the universal destination of the goods of the earth.*[1] Since the earth is a gift to the human community, no member of that community, in principle, has a greater claim on resources than any other member. That is, the fundamental dignity of each human person, as an *imago Dei*, entitles that person to a minimum fair share of the goods of the earth. By the same token, no individual may make an *a priori* claim on a disproportionate share on the grounds of greater personal dignity, such as noble birth. An example in the context of taxation might be the exemption from

1 See the *Compendium of the Social Doctrine of the Church* (hereafter, *CSDC*), nos. 171–84.

certain taxes granted (or widely supposed to have been granted) to French nobility before the Revolution.[2]

At the same time, Catholics believe in a God of abundance, whose gift of the earth is sufficient to sustain the genuine needs of humanity. Human sinfulness being what it is, the Church recognizes that at any given time there is likely to be both waste and a maldistribution of material resources that can be attributed, in part, to human selfishness and fear. The aspiration, however, has always been to achieve a distribution of resources that, if not equal, ensures that no person lacks the necessary material foundation for a minimally decent human life. We will return to this theme later.

The Foundation of the Right to Private Ownership

Some observers have blamed the unequal distribution of resources on the evil of private ownership. The Catholic tradition takes a very different posture. While original sin creates a tendency to selfishness, respect for private ownership helps to ensure that individuals and families can acquire and keep what they need to sustain their lives.[3] It is their right to a share of the earth's goods that generates the right to own property privately. Furthermore, long observation (as Thomas Aquinas noted) confirms the conviction that property owned privately is more likely to be better preserved, better cared for, and used less wastefully.[4]

---

2 The *taille* was an onerous tax levied in France from the end of the fifteenth century to the eighteenth century, which may have contributed at times up to half of the revenues received by the king. Clergy and nobles were generally exempted from this tax, which was a major source of resentment in the period leading up to the Revolution in 1789.

3 Pope Leo XIII, *Rerum Novarum* (1891), nos. 6–10.

4 Thomas Aquinas, *Summa Theologiae*, II–II, q. 66, a. 2.

In the Catholic view, the right to own property is a natural right, not a political right. That is to say, it is a right that attaches to all persons as a consequence of their fundamental human dignity; it is not a right created or granted by civil authority.[5] As a natural right, it cannot be extinguished by civil authority, though it may be regulated.[6] It is also true, as history amply demonstrates, that civil authorities can violate the rights of private persons to own property.

This natural right is ordinarily actualized through human work (though those who cannot work—children, the elderly, or the ill—still have a claim on their fair share).[7] Through their work, human persons become active collaborators with God in the unfolding of creation and rightly appropriate the fruits of the earth to serve their needs. Individuals embrace their personal vocations by developing their gifts (whether material resources, talents, skills, or knowledge) and employing them not only for their own welfare but also for the well-being of others.

5 Pope Leo XIII, *Rerum Novarum* (1891), no. 5; Pope Pius XI, *Quadragesimo Anno* (1931), no. 45; Pope St. John XXIII, *Mater et Magistra* (1961), no. 19; *CSDC*, no. 176.

6 The right of civil authorities to regulate ownership, especially of real property, has led some thinkers to the mistaken view that the general right to own is a creation of the state. As we will see later, this view provides a rationale for a claim that some significant portion of privately held wealth actually belongs to the state, which is entirely free to determine what portion ought to be surrendered on demand.

6 Pope St. John Paul II, *Centesimus Annus* (1991), no. 31; *CSDC*, no. 287.

The Right to Own Property Is Not Absolute

To say that the right to own property is a natural right is not to say that it is without qualifications. The Catholic tradition insists that the right of ownership always entails obligations and is almost always limited in extent.[8] This is expressed in different ways. Sometimes a distinction is made between the right of ownership or possession and the right of use (in which case one might acknowledge the right of owners to possess something but claim that they do not have the right to use their property as they choose). In other texts, the claim is made that ownership has both private and public dimensions (in which case the requirements of the common good may qualify ownership and use). Pope John Paul II famously said that all private property has attached to it a "social mortgage."[9]

However it is expressed, the underlying idea is an extension of the principle of universal destination. Since the Creator made his gift of the earth to the human community, and intended it to benefit each and every person, the right of private ownership must be understood in a way that is consistent with this fundamental principle. There are several implications of this idea.

One is that the right of private ownership must be exercised in such a way as to promote (or at least not impede) a distribution of resources that gives everyone a minimally fair share.[10] For example, since it is possible for some persons to accumulate surplus property, their claim to keep and to use this surplus in the face of the unmet needs of others may be very weak

[8] Pope Pius XI, *Quadragesimo Anno* (1931), nos. 47–51; *CSDC*, nos. 177–78.

[9] Pope St. John Paul II, *Sollicitudo Rei Socialis* (1987), no. 42.

[10] In principle, a minimally fair share would be what is necessary for an individual to pursue his or her vocation and to live a decent life. The contingencies of time and place will result in differences in what this fair share actually is.

or even nonexistent.[11] But, at the same time, civil authorities must respect rights to private ownership and cannot unjustly appropriate the property of the few to benefit the many.

Moreover, the Catholic tradition insists that the wealthy have a solemn moral obligation to use their wealth to meet the urgent needs of others and to support the common good.[12] It also insists that, as a practical matter, the moral obligations of right use cannot be enforced by law. That is to say, the wealthy have a *moral* obligation to make good use of their wealth, especially through acts of generosity and benevolence to benefit the poor. Strictly speaking, though wealth may be taxed, acts of *charity* cannot be compelled by law.[13] (By way of example, recent popes have urged wealthy nations to help developing peoples not merely out of their surplus but also out of their sustenance.)

Still another implication is that the right use of property ought to be shaped by the virtue of *solidarity*. The Catholic tradition understands solidarity to be "a firm and persevering determination to commit oneself to the common good; that is to say to the good of all and of each individual, because we are all really responsible for all."[14] In making decisions about the use of property, persons developing this virtue would consider not only the consequences to themselves and their families but

---

[11] See, for example, St. Thomas Aquinas, *Summa Theologiae*, II–II, q. 66, art. 7, where he argues that, in a situation of great need, a person may take the unused property of another and that such a taking is not theft (because the property owner's claim to his surplus property is overcome by the need of the other).

[12] See, for example, Pope Pius XI, *Quadragesimo Anno* (1931), nos. 50–51, where the pope suggests that investing wealth in enterprises that will provide employment for workers can be an excellent contribution to the common good.

[13] Pope Leo XIII, *Rerum Novarum* (1891), no. 19.

[14] Pope St. John Paul II, *Sollicitudo Rei Socialis* (1987), no. 38.

also the impact of their actions on others, however remote, especially on the poor.

Finally, the right use of property is also governed by what might be called the *principle of proximity*. This moral principle, deeply embedded in Catholic moral theology, stipulates that, other things being roughly equal, persons have stronger obligations to those closer to them than to those more remote (in place or relationship). To be more precise, a person has the greatest moral obligation to meet the needs of his or her immediate family, and then neighbors, fellow citizens, and so on.

This principle would be violated if one were to attend to the needs of individuals in a remote community while one's own family or immediate neighbors went hungry. One has an obligation, for example, to make reasonable provisions for the sheltering and education of one's children even if no additional resources would be left to address the needs of others. At the same time, it should not be understood, contrary to solidarity, as a liberty to lavish luxury on one's family and to be indifferent to the needs of others.

Summary

The right to private ownership is a natural human right, grounded in the material needs of human persons and in God's gift of the earth to all people. This right has qualifications. The requirements of one's personal vocation, the common good, and the unmet needs of other persons, among other factors, impose significant limitations on the exercise of the right to ownership. Nevertheless, within the scope of these limitations, it is legitimate for individuals to acquire ownership of things and ideas and to derive real benefit from this ownership. The state, for its part, has a corresponding duty to respect and protect private ownership, though this duty does not preclude its capacity to demand payments from private members of the community to support legitimate government operations.

Part II

Taxation

VII What Is a Tax?

In one form or another, taxes are as old or older than civilization and government. We do not really know who first levied a tax on the community he governed, but we do know that by the beginning of the third millennium BC taxes were collected by pharaohs and rulers in Mesopotamia. The first form of taxation may have been the corvée, or compulsory contribution of labor to the ruler. As economies developed, taxes were paid not only in labor but in commodities such as grain or livestock, and eventually in money.[1]

There are few things that a ruler or regime takes more seriously than acquiring revenue. Without revenue, the kingdom—or at least the king—cannot survive. Most regimes have had multiple sources of revenue. In primitive communities, the king might claim a significant share of the spoils of war as a principal source of revenue (with predictable consequences for peace between neighbors). In more civilized circumstances, the king would receive revenue from rents and the cultivation of royal lands, from tribute paid by subject peoples, from fines

---

1 See Carolyn Webber and Aaron Wildavsky, *A History of Taxation and Expenditure in the Western World* (New York: Simon & Schuster, 1986) for an excellent survey of the history of taxation in the ancient world.

and penalties, and even from the minting and management of coinage.[2] Needless to say, taxes have taken many forms in five thousand years, such that some payments may look to be taxes but are not, and other payments may not at first appear to be taxes but actually are.[3]

How, then, should we define a tax? Not every payment demanded by government is a tax. (Consider fines and penalties, for example.) Questions of justification or of the range of purposes to which revenue can be devoted or even whether a penalty ought to be considered a tax depend on having an effective definition. Furthermore, this definition ought to be applicable to multiple jurisdictions and respect what obligations people, in different times and places, have thought to be taxes.

Here are a few examples, drawn from different fields. A tax is:

> a pecuniary burden laid upon individuals or property to support the government, and is a payment exacted by legislative authority.[4]

> a charge, usually monetary, imposed by the government on persons, entities, transactions, or property to yield public revenue.[5]

---

2 Blackstone lists twenty-nine different sources of revenue for the king of England. See Blackstone's *Commentaries on the Laws of England* (1765), bk. 1, chap. 8.

3 A notable recent example is the decision by Chief Justice John Roberts, of the Supreme Court of the United States, to recognize the penalty prescribed by the Affordable Care Act for someone who does not purchase medical insurance as a tax after all.

4 *Black's Law Dictionary*, 5th ed. (St. Paul: West Publishing Company, 1979) s.v., "Tax."

5 *Black's Law Dictionary*, 10th ed. (Eagan, MN: Thomson West, 2014), s.v., "Tax."

> enforced proportional contribution from persons and property, levied by the state by virtue of its sovereignty for the support of government and for all public needs.[6]

> a compulsory contribution from the person to the government to defray the expenses incurred in the common interest of all, without reference to special benefits conferred.[7]

> a compulsory contribution to the government, imposed in the common interest of all, for the purpose of defraying the expenses incurred in carrying out the public functions, or imposed for the purpose of regulation, without reference to the special benefits conferred on the one making the payment.[8]

> whatever the subjects or members of the state must contribute for the common usefulness and for the public necessities.[9]

Each of these definitions has some value, and, while some omit or emphasize one characteristic or another, overall they have much in common. Law or economics or political science, as distinct academic fields, may have specific objectives in mind in adopting one definition or another, but it is clear that no

---

6 Thomas M. Cooley, *A Treatise on the Law of Taxation*, 3rd ed. (Chicago: Callaghan & Co., 1903), 1. This definition is very widely cited in texts and cases concerning taxation, though not always properly attributed to Cooley.

7 Edwin R. A. Seligman, *Essays in Taxation* (New York: Macmillan, 1921), 432.

8 Martin T. Crowe, *The Moral Obligation of Paying Just Taxes* (Washington, DC: Catholic University of America Press, 1944), 14–15.

9 Juan de Lugo, *De iustitia et iure* (1670), as quoted in Crowe, *Moral Obligation*, 14.

particular definition is commonly accepted, even within these fields. Therefore, I propose to offer a definition that, while building on these examples, is more comprehensive and, I hope, more suitable to an exploration of ethical issues.

> A tax is *a general obligation imposed in law by proper authority on persons or groups under their jurisdiction, without regard to specific benefits received, that is discharged by the payment of a sum of money or the surrender of property of value to the state or an agent of the state to support the legitimate operations of government.*

Permit me to explain each of the elements.

1. A tax is a *general* obligation. That is, a tax is imposed on a group of persons (e.g., everyone over a certain age who has income above a certain minimum, everyone who purchases a particular item, everyone who engages in a certain activity) rather than specific named individuals or organizations. A payment demanded by law from John Smith, and no one else, or from XYZ Corporation, and no one else, would not be a tax. (And indeed, such a demand for payment might be both unjust and unlawful.)

A tax is also a general *obligation*, as distinct from an invitation to make voluntary contributions to the community. The fact that persons consent to reside in a particular location, even to become citizens of a particular community, and pay the expected taxes without coercion or complaint, does not refute the claim that payment is obligatory. Filing an income tax return and writing a check to the Internal Revenue Service are, in a strict philosophical sense, voluntary acts. They are freely chosen acts, done in voluntary compliance with the law. But in the sense relevant to our definition, they are done out of obedience to the law and under threat of coercive penalties for noncompliance; therefore, the payment of taxes is an obligation.

2. A tax is *imposed in law by proper authority*. Whatever else a tax may be, it is imposed by law by a proper authority, whether that authority is a legislature, an executive, or even a collaboration between the two. A demand for payment not formally enacted or decreed according to law, or lacking proper authority, is not a tax. It is also worth noting that communities other than civil societies may levy and collect taxes, as the Church (which is an ecclesial society) has done and continues to do.

3. A tax is *imposed on persons or groups under their authority*. There may be occasions on which a civil government can demand payments from persons or even other governments that are not under their authority. Examples include reparations for harms caused, compensation for services rendered, or perhaps even some forms of tribute. None of these, however, would be taxes.

4. A tax is imposed *without regard to benefits received*. A common, though not universal, understanding of a tax is that it is not a payment for specific benefits received. One can imagine everything from a payment to government for a temporary parking space or for a government publication to paying an assessment for road work adjoining one's property. Most authorities prefer not to include such payments among taxes as they are more like commercial exchanges or fees.

5. A tax is *discharged by the payment of a sum of money or the surrender of property of value*. In modern economies taxes are almost always paid in money. However, in many cases governments reserve the right to seize real or personal property in satisfaction of tax obligations.

6. A tax is *paid to the state or to an agent of the state*. In the ancient world, and in some cases into modern times, it was common to delegate the collection of taxes to private agents. These agents were obligated to collect a specified amount to be turned over to the government but ordinarily demanded a larger amount from persons subject to the tax. The difference between what they were obligated to surrender to the government and

what they could collect from private persons was income to them. In many communities, tax collectors were especially despised because they employed the threat of the coercive power of the state to collect an oppressive amount from the community and thereby unjustly enrich themselves.[10] Similar opportunities were available to customs agents and others in developed nations earlier in the twentieth century and are still available in some parts of the world.

7. A tax is paid *to support the legitimate operations of government.* A common element of most definitions of a tax is that the revenue collected ought to be used for some public purpose, which could include the operations of government. Of course, this element is problematic because it does not specify which operations would or would not be legitimate. We will return to this issue immediately below and at greater length later. For now, it is sufficient to note that a payment demanded for the aggrandizement of the executive or his cronies is not properly considered a tax (though it might be considered extortion).

So much for the definition of a tax.

We should, however, make mention of general types of taxes within the definition. Taxes can be distinguished on the basis of the levy, on the purpose for the tax, and on whether they discriminate with regard to persons or groups subject to the tax.

Ultimately, taxes are paid by persons, whether they do so directly or indirectly.[11] The basis for calculating the amount of

[10] The story of Zacchaeus in Luke 19:1–10 is meant to be striking because the behavior of Zacchaeus the tax collector is so contrary to common experience.

[11] Taxes are sometimes identified as *direct* or *indirect* but the meanings of these terms vary with context. In some instances, a direct tax is one levied directly on persons or property, such as a capitation or poll tax (not to be mistaken for a tax demanded at a voting place).

the obligation, however, can focus on the person, on property, on an activity, or on income. The point to understand here is that "to tax something" is really to make that something the basis of determining what is owed. In principle, virtually anything could be used as a basis without violating a moral principle. (Though I could imagine some things that would constitute a violation of privacy or be ethically questionable on a similar ground.) Many things that might be used as a basis should be rejected because they would be difficult to measure, would be unstable, would impose burdens unevenly, or would be too easy to avoid.

Direct taxes on persons (capitation) are uncommon in developed economies today, though they were occasionally used in the early history of the United States. (The concept is sometimes used not as a tax but as a means, for example, of determining fees for a contract for medical services where the total is calculated strictly on the basis of the number of persons eligible to receive care under the contract.)

Taxes on real property are, of course, ubiquitous, but broad taxes on personal property are less common. Questions can be raised about whether annual "taxes" on automobiles and boats are really taxes or license fees (and whether license fees should be considered taxes).

Taxes on activities, from sales to adding value at points during a manufacturing process, are quite varied. They raise some ethical issues since they can often be used to manage behaviors in a community (such as taxes on tobacco and alcohol) quite

An indirect tax, then, would be one levied on some activity (such as a sales tax). In other instances, a direct tax is one paid directly by the individual obligated, as perhaps when someone directly pays the property tax on a home. Indirect taxes, in this case, are quite common, and might include any tax where a third party collects the tax on behalf of the person obligated. Examples might include most sales taxes, payroll taxes, and real estate taxes where an escrow is maintained by the agent servicing the mortgage loan.

apart from any intention to raise revenues for general government operations.

Finally, a tax can be levied on income, which levy constitutes the largest single source of revenue for the federal government in the United States. There are, of course, myriad problems in defining income for purposes of calculating tax obligations. The complexity attendant to this is in conflict with Adam Smith's principle that tax obligations should be clear, plain, and certain.[12]

Most of the early definitions of a tax suppose that the purpose of levying a tax is to acquire resources to support the proper operations of the state, though there is generally little discussion offered as to what constitutes these proper operations. The usual assumption is that these operations include such things as the defense of the community from outside enemies (supporting an army and a navy), maintaining internal peace and order (police and a system of courts), and providing for other structures and services of common use (roads, canals, a postal service, and so on). Over the course of the past two centuries. the scope of the operations of a modern state has greatly expanded.[13] An argument is often made that the complexity of modern life demands that government take on a wide variety of responsibilities.[14] Needless to say, a lively discussion continues in the United States over whether the government really ought to be engaged in so many activities—a discussion that is rooted in

---

[12] Adam Smith, *An Inquiry into the Nature and Causes of the Wealth of Nations*, ed. Edwin Cannan (1904), bk. 5, chap. 2, pt. 2. Library of Economics and Liberty, http://www.econlib.org/library/Smith/smWN21.html.

[13] For example, George Washington's first cabinet comprised the vice president, the attorney general, and the secretaries of state, treasury, and war. The modern cabinet comprises fifteen departments.

[14] This argument is made by Pope St. John XXIII in his encyclical *Mater et Magistra* (1961), nos. 59–60.

competing visions about public and private responsibilities in civil societies. We will return to this topic later but for now we can say that taxes are collected to provide general *revenue* to the government (the traditional purpose), to *regulate* behaviors, and to *redistribute* wealth and other benefits.

Finally, taxes may be discriminate or indiscriminate, which is to say that they may vary in their impact based on the particular circumstances of persons or organizations, or they may apply equally to all affected parties regardless of circumstances. Progressive taxation, for instance, discriminates by being unequal in the rate applied, requiring a higher rate from parties with greater resources. Exempting persons or organizations from tax obligations is another way to discriminate. Both forms of discrimination can be just or unjust. Indiscriminate taxes, such as sales taxes or other flat-rate taxes, apply equally to all parties affected. These, too, may be just or unjust. The argument is commonly made that consumption taxes are unjust (that is, regressive) because they impose a disproportionate burden on lower-income individuals. In modern developed societies, however, it is likely that the array of taxes levied by government will include both progressive and regressive forms.

VIII The Authority to Levy Taxes and the Duty to Pay

It cannot be denied that most governments throughout history have had the *power* to levy taxes and to collect revenue from individuals and groups under their jurisdiction. Nor can it be denied that rulers have often employed this power unjustly to favor some persons over others, to extract exorbitant amounts of wealth from their people, to use revenue for evil purposes, and so on. But having determined what a tax is, the question we want to address now is not whether the power to collect revenue is sometimes abused. It is. Instead, we want to inquire into the foundation of the authority of legitimate governments to demand revenue from their people and the corresponding duty of a population to provide that revenue.

Any judgment about whether a tax or a tax rate is just depends to some degree on what we understand to be the formal relationship between taxpayer and government and what we believe the government to be doing when it demands payment. A variety of explanations have been offered. We will consider several of the more important contemporary theories before turning to the construction of an explanation by drawing more explicitly on principles of the social tradition.

Two prominent theories are rooted in opposing claims about the nature of ownership rights.

Where the Right of Ownership Precedes the State

One theory, which we often associate with libertarian thinkers, begins with something like a Lockean account of the foundation of ownership rights.[1] On this account, ownership is a natural right that arises when a person takes possession of an object (which could be land, a moveable object, or even a living thing) and modifies it in some way, putting the stamp of his labor on what will then become his property. For example, think about very primitive situations in which the object of possession is not previously owned. Someone who picks up a stone and fashions it into a cutting tool makes it his property by that action, as does someone who cultivates a plot of land for the first time or tames an animal. The individual who becomes an owner in this way has a moral right to the peaceful possession and use of his property. This does not mean that a stronger and more aggressive individual *cannot* take it away but that such an individual has no right to do this.

The need to secure ownership rights to protect the individual from the predations of others is one of the reasons, on this account, for which governments are initially instituted. But note that these ownership rights are temporally and logically prior to the state, which ought to recognize these rights but does not create them.

Since a legitimate government has duties to perform, it also has a just claim that it holds against those under its jurisdiction (which may include citizens and noncitizens) to the resources necessary for it to do its work. Therefore, it may levy taxes and

---

1 Prominent representatives of libertarian positions are Robert Nozick, *Anarchy, State and Utopia* (New York: Basic Books, 1974) and Murray Rothbard, *The Ethics of Liberty* (New York: New York University Press, 1982). Edward Feser provides an accurate, sympathetic summary of their views on taxation in "Taxation, Forced Labor, and Theft," *The Independent Review* 5, no. 2 (2000), 219–35.

at least some members of the community have a duty to pay.[2] But note that this is principally a duty in commutative justice.[3] Government provides a service (minimally, recognition and protection of ownership rights, but typically much more besides), and those who benefit from the service, potentially or actually, have a duty to pay a fair price for what they receive. Taxes, then, constitute a sort of exchange between buyer (citizen) and seller (government). To put it another way, the beginning assumption is that property owned by private parties truly belongs to them independently of government and that government must offer a compelling reason to demand justly that it receive tax payments.

Because they adopt a rather thin vision of the common good, libertarian authors favor small governments, which offer a limited range of services important to sustain peace and security in the community. They are also inclined to say that the range of government services ought to follow from determinations of what responsible members of the community are willing to pay for; the level of taxes should not be determined by what operations the government independently chooses to pursue.

Two additional concerns are also present in this account. One has to do with the use of force to collect tax payments. The second has to do with the sorts of taxes that can be justified. In particular, authors such as Nozick and Rothbard hold that the taxation of income is an unjust taking.

---

2 We will set aside for the moment questions about who in the community has such a duty—individuals or families, persons with a certain income or wealth, organizations, citizens only, and so on. Different societies may answer these questions differently, but their answers do not affect our discussion of the foundation of the duty.

3 A good account of this, following the work of nineteenth-century French writer Frédéric Bastiat (1801–1850), can be found in Christopher Todd Meredith, "Taxation and Legal Plunder in the Thought of Frédéric Bastiat," *Journal of Markets and Morality* 12, no. 2 (2009): 297–314.

Where the Right of Ownership Is Created by the State

A sharp alternative to the view that government must respect and protect the right of private citizens to own property is the position that, to the contrary, the right of ownership is a creation of the state and cannot exist without the state.[4] We can associate this with an inclination to view society from a collectivist perspective. On this account, individuals may claim a right of ownership and may have some historical foundation for the claim (as Locke might recognize), but the claim is empty without the recognition and protection of the state. Indeed, the existence and operations of the state—police, courts, recorders—provide not the subsequent but rather the initial conditions for ownership rights. In support of this view, one might point to less developed countries where titles to real estate are poorly recorded by government, if at all. In such communities, individuals might occupy and improve land for years or decades only to lose it for lack of title.[5] In what sense, then, can anyone be said to have real rights of ownership without government?

We can go further down this path. Not only is government necessary, initially, for any real ownership rights, it is also the cause of contemporary rights of ownership. What individual or

---

4 A serious and carefully argued defense of a version of this position can be found in Liam Murphy and Thomas Nagel, *The Myth of Ownership* (Oxford: Oxford University Press, 2002). A somewhat more passionate and less tightly argued treatment is Stephen Holmes and Cass R. Sunstein, *The Cost of Rights: Why Liberty Depends on Taxes* (New York: W. W. Norton & Co., 1999).

5 More commonly in such situations, real estate is developed minimally, or not at all, out of a reasonable concern that work and resources invested may be lost at any time and, indeed, improvements in property make it an attractive target for confiscation by government and its allies. Thus, entrepreneurship and the growth of wealth are severely inhibited.

business could create wealth or receive an income without the infrastructure created by government at many levels?[6] We are dependent on government for transportation (roads, railways, canals, ports, airports), for communication (the postal system as well as the regulation of other media), for money as a medium of exchange, for courts to vindicate contracts, for police to enforce the law, and so on. Indeed, not only does government create ownership rights, but also by its laws and regulations it defines precisely what these rights are and has the liberty to change its definitions at will. Therefore, government can define rights

---

6 In August 2011, Harvard professor Elizabeth Warren (later US senator from Massachusetts) said:

> There is nobody in this country who got rich on his own—nobody. You built a factory out there? Good for you. But I want to be clear. You moved your goods to market on the roads the rest of us paid for. You hired workers the rest of us paid to educate. You were safe in your factory because of police-forces and fire-forces that the rest of us paid for.... Now look, you built a factory and it turned into something terrific, or a great idea. God bless—keep a big hunk of it. But part of the underlying social contract is, you take a hunk of that and pay forward for the next kid who comes along.

A year later, in the context of his campaign for a second term as president, Barack Obama famously made a similar claim:

> If you were successful, somebody along the line gave you some help. There was a great teacher somewhere in your life. Somebody helped to create this unbelievable American system that we have that allowed you to thrive. Somebody invested in roads and bridges. If you've got a business—you didn't build that. Somebody else made that happen.

Mr. Obama subsequently corrected his remarks to acknowledge that Americans do indeed build their own businesses.

of ownership in such a way as to justify its claim to resources sufficient to pursue its objectives.

Moreover, on the collectivist view, a market economy may do a fine job of allowing individuals to create wealth but this same system, supported in countless ways by government, also brings about dramatic disparities in the distribution of income and wealth. This is a serious social problem that government has an obligation to remedy by a program of wealth redistribution that may justly use the system of taxation as a vehicle.

A Catholic Alternative

A Catholic account of the authority to levy taxes shares something with both the libertarian and the collectivist accounts. The Catholic tradition, as we have seen, vigorously supports the right of private ownership as a natural right, not a creature of the state. But the tradition also rejects the thin version of the common good that libertarians propose, along with their tendency to regard human persons as isolated by nature rather than being profoundly social.

We might note that both the libertarian and the collectivist claims about the right to levy taxes come down to a matter of *commutative* justice. For the libertarian, taxes are fair payment for services rendered, whether those services are actually needed (e.g., roads, currency) or just available if the need arises (e.g., fire departments, courts). For the collectivist, taxes are just compensation for the state's creation and protection of rights of ownership. Or, in other cases, they may be just restitution for the real but (perhaps) unintended harms created by the activities of the marketplace.

When it comes to the question of the authority of the state to levy taxes, the Catholic tradition appeals first to the responsibility of the state to sustain and protect the common goods (both instrumental and substantive) of the society. As a matter of principle, no one can be morally obligated to perform a duty, as civil authorities are so bound, unless the necessary resources are made available. Civil authorities, then, have a claim on someone and that someone is obviously a subset of the members of the community.[7]

Given their responsibility to order the community in support of the common good, civil authorities have a duty, under the rubric of legal justice, to enact legislation that provides for the revenue needs of the state. But the particular form this legislation takes must itself honor the common good. It must respect limits for government operations and not seek revenues for inappropriate objectives. It cannot create unnecessary distortions in economic and social life. It must apply the rules of distributive justice in apportioning duties to pay.

For their part, members of the community have a duty in legal justice to accept reasonable legislation about taxes peacefully and to comply in good time. The legislation enacted may be imperfect, it may not be the best alternative available, and it may impose real sacrifices on some members of the community. Nevertheless, in legal justice, as long as the plan is reasonable (with considerable latitude given to this judgment) and it com-

[7] It is true that, in other times and places, the state was expected to fund its comparatively limited operations from sources other than taxing citizens. These sources commonly included income derived from land belonging to the king (there was a reason it was called *real* estate), from excise taxes, from tariffs on imported goods, from tribute paid by conquered or nervous neighbors, and so on. The rise of the welfare state in the nineteenth century, the ambitions of the Progressive movement, and the complexity of life in the twentieth century combined to prompt, at the national level, more direct modes of taxing citizens, such as the income tax and various sales or value-added taxes. See, as an example, Randolph E. Paul, "History of Taxation in the United States," *Proceedings of the First Annual Tax Conference* 1 (1955): 5–16.

plies in other respects with the requirements for a just law, it is morally binding. Taxpayers may argue for a better scheme—and they may even be right—but until a better scheme is properly enacted, they are still obligated in justice to submit to the law.

IX Purposes Served by Levying Taxes

There are four basic questions that must be addressed in relation to the justice of tax policies: (1) for what purposes may taxes be levied, (2) what forms of tax may be employed, (3) how should the burden of paying taxes be distributed among those who have a duty to pay, and (4) who may rightly be exempt from paying taxes. This section will consider the first question.

Any judgment about the purposes that may be served by taxation is rooted in convictions about the proper role of the government in society. It goes without saying that there are various ways to think about this question. Many of these approaches seem self-evidently reasonable to their proponents, but, in fact, most are rooted in philosophical positions long since forgotten—positions that may not stand close examination. We will not attempt to survey the field here but instead will offer some thoughts about how the understanding of the state in the Catholic social tradition may shape our views about tax policies.

The starting point is to recall that human life in society is, in fact, much larger than the proper scope of government action in at least three dimensions. First, there is the private life of individuals, centered on the family but including other relationships as well. Second, there is the cultural life of the community—including its intellectual and aesthetic activities as well as a history and a range of customs—which grounds and perpetuates the identity of the community. (This dimension gives shape to the state in the end.) And third, there is a spiritual dimension that is the proper sphere of the Church. The history of practical politics is, in large part, a history of the tensions among these dimensions and the challenges of defining their boundaries. Tax policies will inevitably be shaped by the ways in which we draw these boundaries and the respect we show them once drawn.

Taxes may rightly be levied to support any legitimate activity of government, including appropriate compensation for government officials and employees. Broadly speaking, taxes seem to be levied in modern societies for three general purposes: to raise revenue for the support of government operations, to regulate otherwise lawful private choices (either to encourage or to discourage), and to redistribute wealth among members of the society.[1] We will consider each one in turn.

Legitimate Government Operations

As we have noted before, the principal objective of government is in the natural order, and this is to sustain, defend, and perfect (as far as possible) the instrumental common good of society. To put it another way, the warrant of civil authorities to act in society is limited to fulfilling their responsibilities to the common good. They have an obligation, sometimes made explicit in positive law, to avoid encroaching on the private, cultural, and spiritual life of the community—except insofar as it is necessary to secure the common good. From this it follows that there are some generic operations or responsibilities that are proper to

1 These purposes roughly correspond to the three views on the taxing power described in a classic article by Robert E. Cushman, "The National Police Power under the Taxing Clause of the Constitution," *Minnesota Law Review* 4 (March 1920): 247–81.

the state, others that may rightly be delegated to the state, and yet others from which civil authorities ought to refrain.[2]

Proper state operations include the obvious: (1) legislative activities, (2) executive activities, including exercise of police power, (3) judicial activities in both criminal and civil spheres, and (4) military activities in defense of the community from external threats.[3] Stable governments throughout history have displayed these functions at minimum, though all four may not be present at all levels of government.

Other operations that are commonly performed by government include (1) issuance of currency, (2) the regulation of commerce and markets, (3) construction and maintenance of transportation infrastructure, and (4) at least some rudimentary form of public communication. No doubt more examples could be added. In the case of operations like these, however, it is much more likely that private parties would also be engaged in parallel functions. Banks create credit, specific markets often create their own rules, private parties build roads and bridges, and private modes of communication now threaten to drive public postal services out of business. Societies, however, for good reason

2 An operation is "proper" to the state when it follows from the reason for the state's being and is necessary for achieving its aim. For example, the legislative function follows immediately from the objective of the state to direct citizens to support the common good. To form a government necessarily empowers civil authorities to legislate.

3 Advocates of minimal government sometimes make the argument that many, perhaps all, of these activities could be privatized. There is some truth to this. Some legislation could be replaced by contracts, some policing could be replaced by private security, courts by private arbitration, and armies by mercenaries. Nevertheless, these activities, even if not exclusive to government (though history seems to show that substitution by the private sectors in these areas generally does not work well) are still proper to it.

have often preferred to make government principally responsible for providing services like this that benefit the general public. There are, of course, always projects that seek to use public funds to the benefit of a small, if indeterminate, segment of the community. In the United States, the use of public money to construct massive and expensive stadiums for professional sports teams has often been controversial. Without ruling out the possibility of their legitimacy, one can reasonably wonder whether the common good is truly served in such projects.

We can also speak about a range of operations that, strictly speaking, are not *proper* to government. Until the modern era, they were at best only a small part of state operations but have now become common features of government in developed societies. We might call these *delegated* operations because they tend to follow from deliberate decisions of citizens and legislative bodies to assign responsibility to the state for these functions in whole or in part. These could include education, healthcare, welfare, social insurance, and many more.[4]

Finally, we can identify a set of operations that intrude on the other dimensions and, apart from exceptional circumstances, should not be taken on by government. These would include the inclinations, by definition, of totalitarian governments to bring family, culture, and religion under the control of the state, which the Catholic tradition simply rejects. They would

---

4 There is an interesting history to be written about how these functions came to be commonly regarded as government responsibilities. One of the starting points of that history would be the creation of the social welfare state in Germany under Bismarck in the nineteenth century. It is worth noting, at least, that the movement to assign these functions to government was in part also a movement to wrest them away from the Church, which had been very active in each of the areas mentioned.

also include instances of what Pope St. John Paul II called "substitute functions."[5]

The legitimacy of the proper operations of the state is not an issue. For the other categories, some general principles are helpful. The overriding principle is that the operations of the state must serve the common good. Activities that use public monies for private benefits or situations in which risk is socialized and reward is privatized probably fail this test and therefore would not be suitable purposes for levying taxes.

A second principle is subsidiarity, which discourages civil authorities from interfering in the proper activities of families, other private bodies, and the Church unless intervention is necessary to promote the common good.[6] An effort, for example, to exclude private associations or the Church from providing relief to the poor, and substituting their efforts with publicly funded programs would probably violate this principle.[7]

---

5 See Pope St. John Paul II, *Centesimus Annus* (1991), nos. 11, 48–49. "Such supplementary interventions, which are justified by urgent reasons touching the common good, must be as brief as possible, so as to avoid removing permanently from society and business systems the functions which are *properly* theirs and so as to avoid enlarging excessively the sphere of state intervention to the detriment of both economic and civil freedom" (no. 48, emphasis added). See also Pope Leo XIII, *Rerum Novarum* (1891), no. 29: "in [some] cases there can be no question that, within certain limits, it would be right to call in the help and authority of the law. The limits must be determined by the nature of the occasion which calls for the law's interference—the principle being this, that the law must not undertake, nor go further, than is required for the remedy of the evil or the removal of danger."

6 State intervention to prevent or remedy injustice, or to protect vulnerable persons from harm, serves the common good and is legitimate, though it ought to be narrowly targeted.

7 The Church has no objection in principle to the state's assuming a variety of welfare functions. Indeed, some voices in the tradition

A third principle, however, is that citizens should have considerable freedom in determining which functions to assign to government. It is quite legitimate for one nation to make such functions as energy generation and distribution, transportation (i.e., airlines and railroads), communication (i.e., radio, television, and newspapers) entirely private enterprises, while another nation may choose to make some or all of them government activities.

Finally, in any society but perhaps especially in a democracy, every temptation to corruption of any sort must be avoided. Legislators must avoid direct efforts to suborn their roles, obviously, but they must also be mindful of more subtle and indirect pressures. These could include lobbying efforts that seek benefits for one group while transferring costs to the taxpaying population that has no voice in the discussion other than the legislators themselves.

Regulatory Taxation

In addition to obtaining funding for their legitimate operations, civil authorities sometimes use their power to tax to influence otherwise lawful private behaviors or to collect revenue to be used to offset the public expenses incurred by these behaviors. In general, we can speak of this as regulatory taxation.[8] This form of taxation is often used where other government powers, such as the police power, seem to be ineffective or inefficient. The most prominent lesson in American history may be the

affirm a need in the modern world for the state to do just that. (See, for example, Pope St. John XXIII, *Pacem in Terris* [1963], no. 64) At the same time, however, the Church insists that the exercise of charity is an essential element of its life and cannot be abandoned. (See Pope St. John Paul II, *Centesimus Annus* [1991], no. 49 and Pope Benedict XVI, *Deus Caritas Est* [2005], nos. 29–34.

8 An older but excellent study is R. Alton Lee, *A History of Regulatory Taxation* (Lexington: University Press of Kentucky, 1973).

failed experiment in prohibiting the production and sale of alcoholic beverages (1920–1933). This has led some people to propose abandoning the policy of criminalizing the sale and possession of many nontherapeutic drugs in favor of managing the problem through regulation and taxation.

Regulatory taxation may be more common on local and state levels than on the national level, but it could include so-called sin taxes, or, generally, taxes on consumption behavior that government wishes to discourage. The key distinction is that the government does not intend to recover costs imposed on the community by private behaviors but rather to raise the costs of these choices for private persons.[9] The revenue produced will be used for other purposes, but the project would be unsuccessful if there were not significant changes in behavior, regardless of revenues. Elevated excise taxes on gasoline, principally intended to reduce consumption, or high tariffs on specific imported products, either to discourage their purchase or to protect domestic producers, also fall into this category. Still another example would be taxes levied on the purchase of expensive "gas-guzzling" cars.

At the same time, tax preferences can be used to encourage the purchase of certain products. In recent years, a federal tax credit has been available to purchasers of approved electric vehicles, such as certain Tesla models. Preferences such as accelerated depreciation have often been used to encourage capital purchases in some industries, while others have attempted to encourage employment, corporate relocation, or even motion picture production in specific locations.

---

9 Regulatory taxation needs to be distinguished from taxes on private consumption or other activities that are used to fund government operations related to those activities. An example would be a tax on gasoline consumption where the revenue is used to fund highway maintenance and construction.

In both instances, whether the tax is intended to discourage or to encourage private, lawful behaviors, two moral principles may come into play. First, as with taxation for revenue, regulatory taxation must serve the common good. It loses its legitimacy to the extent that it merely reflects private preferences or prejudices, or that it seeks to reform a segment of the population (consumers of soft drinks, for example), or that in fact it fails to serve the common good. In this respect, legislators have a duty to ensure that in imposing a regulatory tax they take into account all of the effects of the tax, not merely the impact on one variable.[10]

Second, regulatory taxation that aims at encouraging behaviors often has the effect of transferring costs forcibly to one portion of the population for the benefit of another. For example, the federal tax credit of as much as $7,500 that was offered to purchasers of electric vehicles entailed imposing an offsetting cost across the population of taxpayers. If the common good is truly served by this transfer (the direct benefits of which were available, in fact, only to purchasers who could afford the high cost of the cars), then reasonable and well-informed taxpayers could be assumed to favor it, and their congressional representatives would have acted justly in voting for the tax. On the other hand, if the tax actually had little real public benefit—the real benefit going to purchasers and manufacturers—then reasonable and well-informed taxpayers would have objected and the

[10] R. Alton Lee, *A History of Regulatory Taxation*, describes nineteenth-century efforts to curb the consumption of oleomargarine through regulatory taxation. The efforts had multiple intentions including protection of the dairy industry and ensuring public safety in the face of a new product. They were successful in discouraging consumption well into the twentieth century, but they had an unintended consequence: imposing higher costs on low-income families. In any event, public safety concerns were exaggerated and real questions can be asked about whether the common good was genuinely served.

transfer would have been forced (that is, it would have happened against their will). Similarly, other taxes (such as tariffs) that benefit a small group rather than the common good, are morally objectionable.

A further observation is that regulatory taxation may seek to obtain restitution from the subjects of the tax for costs (externalities) imposed on the community by the behaviors taxed. So, a tax on cigarettes might not only be intended to discourage the behavior (and might arguably promote the common good in various ways) but it might also be intended to recover some of the costs that smoking imposes on the community. These might include costs of healthcare, loss of productivity due to sickness, and so on. In such circumstances, if the intent of the tax, at least in part, is truly to serve the common good and the revenue obtained is actually used for that purpose, the tax can be justified.

Taxation to Remedy and Redistribute

We live in a world of inequalities, which has been true of every society we know, in every culture, over a span of more than four millennia. Some of the inequalities are natural—differences in intelligence, talent, and health. Others are matters of chance—differences in discovery, fortune, and opportunity. But some are indeed the result of injustices. No society in history has succeeded in eliminating these inequalities and most have not tried to do so. Some, for brief periods, have made the attempt, with disappointing and occasionally disastrous results. The issue we turn to now is whether it is necessary, or even morally permissible, for civil authorities in modern developed economies to use their authority to levy taxes to remedy some of these inequalities, especially inequalities in the distribution of wealth.[11]

There are well-developed arguments supporting a number of responses to this question.[12] On the interventionist side, proponents commonly argue along the following lines: It is a fundamental duty of the modern state to ensure, as far as may be possible, the actual well-being of all members of the community. This requires that members of the community actually have the minimum resources and opportunities necessary to permit them to pursue their vision of a good life. However, the political and economic conditions of modern life, some of which have been set in place by the state (such as laws favoring industrial capitalism and private ownership), prevent many members of the community from acquiring the resources they need, while giving some others far more than they need. Moreover, the conditions that permit some persons to acquire great wealth are also creations of the state, without whose actions this concentra-

---

[11] I frame the question rather narrowly because the topic could easily (mis)lead us into a far larger arena of political philosophy and economics concerning the general role of the state in the modern world. I specifically want to focus on the use of tax money to redistribute wealth rather than the much broader question of whether tax receipts should be used to address the whole array of inequalities that may arise in a society.

[12] Some examples of classic texts include, on the interventionist side, John Rawls, *Justice as Fairness* (Cambridge: Harvard University Press, 2001); Michael J. Sandel, *Liberalism and the Limits of Justice* (Cambridge: Cambridge University Press, 1982); and Liam Murphy and Thomas Nagel, *The Myth of Ownership* (Oxford: Oxford University Press, 2002). On the noninterventionist side, there is F. A. Hayek, *The Mirage of Social Justice*, vol. 2 of *Law, Legislation and Liberty* (London: Routledge & Kegan Paul, 1976); Bertrand de Jouvenal, *The Ethics of Redistribution* (Cambridge: Cambridge University Press, 1952); and Robert Nozick, *Anarchy, State, and Utopia* (New York: Basic Books, 1974).

tion (or maldistribution) of wealth would not be possible. So, even if the wealth of the few was acquired without deliberate injustice, the state still has a warrant to take some of it through taxation and distribute it to others in the community in order to reduce inequalities.

On the noninterventionist side, proponents offer alternate arguments: The fundamental duty of the state is not to ensure the actual well-being of members of the community but rather to secure peace and to guarantee the freedom of its members to pursue their vision of a good life. This exercise of freedom, for a variety of reasons, will result in inequalities. Some people will be fabulously successful and others will fail, possibly through no fault of their own. Some will work hard and some will be lazy. It is not the duty of the state to remedy this situation, but it is the duty of the state to prevent or remedy injustices in the exercise of freedom. If persons have acquired wealth unjustly, for example, the state may require them to make restitution and may also impose penalties. Beyond this, the state has a duty to respect the rights of private ownership and may not take wealth justly acquired simply to redistribute it.

I suggest that the Catholic social tradition has some sympathy for both positions but is not in full agreement with either.

To begin, the fundamental purpose of the state is to secure the instrumental common good of society; the fact that it is instrumental means that it is not a set of results but a set of conditions that would favor certain results. To offer a poor analogy, this is the difference between ensuring that a baseball game is played fairly and ensuring that both teams are evenly matched in every respect. Part of the state's duty, then, is also to ensure that its own actions (laws, regulations, and so forth) do not unnecessarily impede some members of the community or favor others. If this is discovered to be a consequence of state action, it should be remedied.

Furthermore, it is obvious that many natural inequalities will persist in society, but these need not be regarded as a problem to be solved. Instead, differences may be opportunities for collaboration and exchange. And those who are blessed with greater gifts, of whatever kind, are reminded of the duties that accompany those gifts.[13] The right to own is not the same as the right to use in any way one wishes; the right to own great wealth entails solemn duties to use it well. In this regard, the tradition would remind us that wealth is rarely hoarded but is instead spent (sometimes unwisely), taxed for other purposes, invested, and donated to a variety of institutions.[14] The Church greatly encourages beneficence and charity.

The tradition is also willing to acknowledge that modern economic systems have produced tremendous benefits and have lifted billions of people out of abject poverty. However, there are many who remain behind while others experience a sort of super-development, which surrounds them with material resources but often leaves them blind to spiritual needs.[15] We should appreciate the successes but also continue to seek effective ways to include everyone in their benefits.

Finally, whatever the state may do to secure the common good, it must respect the right of private ownership. The right to own is not a creation of the state, even if some forms of property do depend upon state action. Property and wealth acquired

---

13 See, for example, Pope Leo XIII, *Rerum Novarum* (1891), nos. 18–19.

14 Note Pope Pius XI, *Quadragesimo Anno* (1931), nos. 50–51, where the pope reminds people who have "superfluous wealth" of their duty to use it well and then immediately suggests that investing this wealth in enterprises that create employment would be an excellent use of it.

15 See Pope St. John Paul II, *Sollicitudo Rei Socialis* (1987), nos. 17–19, 28.

justly may not be taken without compensation, except perhaps in situations of extreme emergency.[16] Therefore, the state may not simply acquire private wealth by levying a tax for the purpose of redistribution. However, it can and should encourage wealthy persons to perform acts of generosity and benevolence. It may, and generally does, provide tax preferences for certain sorts of gifts as incentives. It is also true that citizens can delegate to the state the right to levy taxes in order to provide relief to persons in need and to subsidize opportunities for them.

16 In France in the 1780s, a small minority of persons (including the Church), owned much of the wealth of the country. Taxes were high and crushing on the relatively poor majority and the wealthy did little to relieve their situation. Things came to a head in 1789 following an agricultural crisis, and a bloody revolution was the result. In similar conditions, with a great disparity of wealth, a rise of envy, and little generosity from the wealthy, civil authorities might rightly consider that some redistribution was necessary in order to prevent great civil unrest, that is, to protect the common good.

X Calculating and Distributing Tax Burdens

My intention in this section is to consider some ethical questions related to choices about tax levies; I will not consider questions of efficiency and other aspects of public policy.

The authority to levy taxes is made effective by a plan. The plan, enacted into law, identifies the object of the tax (what is to be taxed), the measure (rate) to be applied to the object, and, in the first instance at least, the person or group who will bear the burden of the tax. Though actual tax levies are rarely simple, in general, a tax levy is simply a means of calculating and distributing a burden across a segment of a population. The ethical questions involved are issues of distributive and legal justice, but we can also identify several specific issues that deserve attention.

How Much Money Does Government Need?

I submit that the first question we need to ask concerning a tax levy is not "How much can the population afford to pay?" or "How much can government collect without harming the economy significantly?" but rather "How much does the government need?" In two of the very few public comments the popes made about taxation in the twentieth century, Pope Pius XII addressed this issue.

> The financial needs of each of the nations, large or small, have tremendously increased. The fault is due not only to international complications or tensions. It is due also, and perhaps much more, to the huge increase in the State's activity. This activity, dictated too often by false or unhealthy ideologies, makes of financial policy and particularly of taxation policy an instrument serving preoccupations of quite different order.

He continued by urging his audience of public finance officials to

> forego those measures which, despite their technical virtuosity, shock and wound the people's sense of the just and unjust, or which relegate to the background their vital urge, their legitimate ambition to harvest the fruits of their own labor, and their anxiety over family security, all considerations which merit first place in the mind of the legislator and not the last.
>
> The financial system of the State should aim at reorganizing the economic situation in a manner that would assure the people the material conditions of life indispensable for following the supreme end assigned by the Creator: the development of intellectual, spiritual and religious life.
>
> As for you, your high ability calls you to defend financial policy against the maneuvers of the ambitious and the demagogues.[1]

1 Pope Pius XII, "On Public Finance" (Address to delegates at the Congress of the International Institute of Public Finance, 2 October 1948). Translation from *The Catholic Mind* (March 1949): 189–90.

He returned to the issue several years later.

> There can be no doubt concerning the duty of each citizen to bear a part of the public expense. It is the obligation of the State, however—insofar as it is charged with protecting and promoting the common good of citizens—to assess upon its citizens only necessary levies which are, furthermore, proportionate to their means. Taxation can never become, then, a convenient way for public authority to make up a deficit brought on by an improvident administration, or a means of favoring one industry or branch of business at the expense of another of equal utility.
>
> Modern states tend today to multiply their interventions and to make themselves answerable for an increasing number of services; they exercise tighter control over the economy; they intervene to a greater extent in the social protection of many classes of workers. Thus their need for money mounts in proportion to the degree to which they enlarge their administrations. Excessively heavy impositions often oppress private initiative, check the development of industry and commerce, and work to the detriment of good will.
>
> It can be said, in short, that the great size of present-day states points up the need for a carefully worked out program of fiscal legislation. This legislation is still encumbered, in more than one respect, by a questionable empiricism. It is of the upmost importance, moreover, that the moral principles justifying taxation be equally clear to the governing and those governed and that they be effectively applied.[2]

---

2 Pope Pius XII, "On Taxes" (Address to the International Association for Financial and Fiscal Law, 3 October 1956). Translation from *The Pope Speaks* (Summer 1957), 77–80.

Clearly, the pope was persistently concerned about unwarranted growth in the demands of the state for revenue. He was certainly willing to acknowledge the proper functions of the state, but at the same time he was concerned, as the tradition has always been, that the operations of the state must be at the service of the common good. This translates into a certain humility, both about what state action can accomplish, with its "technical virtuosity," and about how many of the imperfections of (sinful) societies government can effectively address.[3]

The popes wish to see a sort of balance achieved between the perceived needs of the state for revenue and respect for private ownership. Unless we can have a fairly high level of confidence that the state can use resources well in service of the common good, properly conceived, it may be better to leave resources in the hands of individuals and families. Legislators have a solemn duty in this regard to resist "the ambitious and the demagogues," and anyone driven more by ideology or private interest (these could include activists and corporations) and exercise prudence and justice in establishing tax policies. In this regard, they might well be guided by the old medical principle, *primum non nocere*, first do no harm. They should avoid costly experiments with public funds and insist that programs be reviewed to ensure that they achieve objectives in service of the common good.

---

[3] While the Church does call on government to address social needs, it generally does so under the rubric of the state's duty to the common good. It sees a legitimate role for the state but also worries that temporary interventions tend to become permanent and that the state tends to expand its operations, crowding out other, nonstate organizations. See, for example, Pope St. John Paul II, *Sollicitudo Rei Socialis* (1987), nos. 36–40, and *Centesimus Annus* (1991), no. 48.

What Aggregate Burden Can the Community Support without Undermining the Common Good?

Assuming a prudent and realistic estimate of the revenue requirements of government has been made, we can inquire into the capacity of the community to bear the burden of satisfying those requirements. The responsibility to make this determination in the concrete falls ultimately on legislators and is a duty of legal justice. Several considerations are important here.

First, legislators need to be mindful of the aggregate tax burden, which would include federal, state, and local levies on the full spectrum of taxable objects: property, income, sales, and so on. A single levy, considered in isolation, may be only a minor burden, but that same levy, when added to all the others binding an individual, may be onerous indeed. In nations with federated political structures, such as the United States, it is often difficult, if not impossible, to coordinate tax levies enacted at different levels and in different jurisdictions. Being mindful of the meaning of the common good, aggregate levels of taxation should not be permitted to reach a point at which they seriously retard economic activity at the cost of jobs, goods, and investment.

Second, legislators have a duty to ensure that the whole burden of taxation falling on citizens is "proportionate to their means."[4] This includes not only the aggregate burden but also the particular burden falling on individuals and families. Legislators need to attend to the problem of cost shifting. In the end, it is always persons or groups (especially families) who pay taxes.

4 Note also the comment of Pope Leo XIII, *Rerum Novarum* (1891), no. 35: "The right to possess private property is from nature, not from man; and the State has only the right to regulate its use in the interests of the public good but by no means to abolish it altogether. The State is, therefore, unjust and cruel, if, in the name of taxation, it deprives the private owner of more than is just."

Assigning a tax to an organization does not mean that the burden remains with that organization; quite often it is passed on to individual customers or employees in the form of higher prices or lower wages. And in many cases, the individuals who ultimately bear the burden are among those least able to bear it easily.

Third, the common good is served not only by framing tax policies that enhance (or at worst, minimally distort) the economic life of the community; it also requires attention to the health of that society within society—the family. From the Church's perspective, an economy is not an economy of individuals but an economy of families.[5] In shaping the economy, legislators need to consider not only macroeconomic issues but also the protection and support of families, both those in distress and those working to order their lives well.

Finally, for our purposes, legislators have a duty to budget prudently, not only for the short term but also for the long-term welfare of the community. This means, among other things, giving attention to the impact of today's decisions on the taxpayers of the future. They cannot assume that wars and other unpredictable events never happen and thus fail to budget for emergencies. They must resist easy promises made today that will impose unfunded burdens on the future.[6] Failure to correct these mistakes will put civil authorities precisely in the position

[5] Note, for example, the Church's defense of the right of private ownership as entailed by the duty of parents to care for their families, as in Pope Leo XIII, *Rerum Novarum* (1891), nos. 9–10; and the importance of a family wage, as in Pope Piux XI, *Quadragesimo Anno* (1931), no. 71.

[6] A dramatic contemporary example is the collection of pension obligations at the state level in the United States. Common estimates place unfunded obligations—which, if honored, would be a burden on younger generations—in the range of $2–3 trillion, or more.

described by Pope Pius XII, wherein they will be tempted to increase tax revenues in order "to make up a deficit brought on by [their] improvident administration."

What May Legitimately Be the Objects of a Tax Levy?

If we think of a tax levy as a means of calculating the share of the burden of supporting the government that ought to fall to each eligible individual or family, then there is nothing, in principle, that could not be the object of measurement. We need not think of something as falling under a negative judgment because it is the object of a tax calculation. Early tax levies tended to be quite simple. Capitation was common, where the burden was measured by counting the number of "heads," or people, in a household. Or the number of livestock could be counted as a measure of wealth and capacity to pay. Virtually anything could be chosen.[7] Of course, some objects were in fact chosen in order to discourage behaviors or to burden more heavily some members of the community. Nevertheless, the imagination of legislators in enacting tax levies has been virtually boundless.

But at the same time, the imagination of taxpayers seeking to avoid tax obligations has been even more creative.[8] Tax windows, and taxpayers will board them up. Tax beards, and they will shave. Tax land, and they will dispute the value. Tax income, and some of it will be concealed. The game is endless—but it

7 For example, in the Middle Ages and the early modern period, a "hearth tax" or "chimney tax" was employed in various countries, partly because it was easier to count the number of chimneys than the number of people in a household. After the seventeenth century, both England and France employed a "window tax," which assessed households for the number of windows in their homes.

8 John Maynard Keynes is alleged to have said: "The avoidance of taxes is the only intellectual pursuit that still carries any reward."

must be played. Something, or some things, must be the object of measurement in order to apportion tax burdens. Over the past couple of centuries, first the British and then the Americans, settled on a tax on income, offered as a superior alternative to property taxes and tariffs. (One wonders if the early advocates of an income tax, first permanently adopted in the United States after 1913, had any inkling of how complicated the measurement of income would be.) Of course, on state and local levels, sales and real estate, among other things, continue to be objects of taxation. No doubt, in the future, new objects will be devised, as for example a tax on e-mail messages (measured by number of messages or quantity of data).

The Catholic social tradition has virtually nothing directly to say about the legitimate objects of taxation. Instead, we can infer from the tradition that some objects would be inappropriate because of the secondary effects of taxing them. For example, it would be unwise to impose special taxes on something like bread as a basic foodstuff. Prices would rise and households on tight budgets would find a disproportionate amount of their income spent on food. The same would follow from taxes on any other basic necessity: clothing, energy, medicine, and so on. While it would not be immoral in principle to make any of these items objects of a tax calculation, it may be unjust in fact if it makes it more difficult for low-income households to live a minimally decent life. Similarly, it may be unjust to make a critical raw material the object of a tax levy if doing so would cause significant and otherwise unnecessary economic disruption.

All this being said, there is no reason to suppose that anything is naturally immune from taxation, or, for that matter, that anything is a natural object. Some things should be avoided because their use would be likely to involve injustice in distributing burdens or entail particular difficulties in accurate measurement. Other things are reasonably preferred because the principles of distributive justice are more easily applied to them or simply because measurement is more efficient and more accurate.

Discrimination in Tax Levies

Perhaps the most persistent question concerning justice in taxation has to do with whether it is unjust to discriminate between taxpayers in determining concrete obligations to pay. The question takes concrete form in several ways. Most commonly, we may ask whether it is just to reduce or even to eliminate a duty to pay a tax for persons or households with a significantly lower than average income (or very little wealth). When this is done, we usually speak of the tax policy as "progressive." We can also ask whether it is just to demand that persons or households with a much higher than average income (or greater wealth) pay a disproportionately greater amount in tax. And finally, we can ask whether it is just to demand the same tax payment from all persons and households, regardless of their income or wealth.

In fact, in the United States, all three possibilities are in play as part of the aggregate tax burden. The federal income tax levy, for example, significantly reduces the tax burden on lower income taxpayers and increases it on those with higher incomes.[9] At the same time, state and local taxes on, say, sales

9 To toss some data into the discussion by way of illustration: According to the Tax Foundation, in 2014, the top 1 percent of federal tax filers in the United States received just under 21 percent of all income reported. They paid over 39 percent of all federal income tax receipts, with an average rate of about 27 percent. On the other hand, the bottom 50 percent of tax filers that year received just over 11 percent of all income reported. They accounted for less than 3 percent of all federal income tax receipts, with an average rate of 3.45 percent. At the federal level, personal income tax receipts account for about 50 percent of revenue. Corporate tax receipts contribute another 10 percent, with tariffs and customs

or real property may in some jurisdictions be mitigated for lower income taxpayers by refund programs that effectively reduce the out-of-pocket expense. On the other hand, an array of taxes, from payroll taxes to taxes on one's telephone bill to "sin taxes" on tobacco and alcohol are levied without discrimination. These taxes are commonly called regressive.[10]

The presence of reduced demands, increased demands, and absolute equality of demand in the aggregate tax policies of the country might reasonably cause us to wonder whether all three can be justified. The Catholic social tradition has rarely addressed the question of progressivity, but it might neverthe-

---

excise taxes (once the largest source of federal revenue) contributing only about 4 percent. Retrieved at: https://taxfoundation.org/summary-latest-federal-income-tax-data-2016-update/.

10 For more than a century there has been a lively discussion and an abundance of scholarly articles about the best form and proper justification for progressive taxation, though in recent decades the practice has been so peacefully accepted that the discussion has tended to focus on how much progression is desired, and less on why it ought to be done. A classic and exhaustive article on the arguments for progression is Elmer D. Fagan, "Recent and Contemporary Theories of Progressive Taxation," *Journal of Political Economy* 46, no. 4 (1938): 457–98. Another classic is Walter J. Blum and Harry Kalven, Jr, "The Uneasy Case for Progressive Taxation," *University of Chicago Law Review* 19 (1952): 417–520 (later reprinted as a small book). A libertarian critique is Murray N. Rothbard, "The Uneasy Case for Degressive Taxation: A Critique of Blum and Kalven," *The Quarterly Journal of Economics* 4, no. 1 (2001): 43–61. In 1995, two careful essays appeared that argue opposite sides of the question. Donna M. Byrne favors progressivity in "Progressive Taxation Revisited," *Arizona Law Review* 37 (1995): 739–89. Jeffrey A. Schoenblum, on the other hand, argues for equality of tax burdens in "Tax Fairness or Unfairness? A Consideration of the Philosophical Bases for Unequal Taxation of Individuals," *American Journal of Tax Policy* 12 (1995): 221–71.

less offer us three tools for dealing with the problem. The first two are very general principles or observations, while the third is more specific in application.

First, the tradition understands justice above all to be a quality, a virtue, of persons. Part of the reason for this is that, given the messiness of human life, especially of sinful human life, situations are often created in society in which it is practically impossible to sort out with precision what justice requires.[11] In such cases—and they are more common than we might think—the practical solution is to fall back on the judgment of a truly just person. What does he or she think is the best way to move forward? Can some resolution be found that approximates justice sufficiently to satisfy most, if not all, parties?

This can be applied to the issue of taxation. For many reasons, it may be impossible as a matter of policy to determine precisely what an individual's just share of the burden ought to be. The best we can do is a reasonable approximation of what justice requires, which is precisely the responsibility of the legislator, as a duty in legal justice.

A second observation is that what people have come to accept peacefully over time as a just resolution of an issue, or a just policy, is a reasonable approximation of justice. There are principles in both civil and canon law, for example, that hold that an (apparent) abrogation of law, if it has been tolerated without challenge for a period of years, may take on the force of law. Similarly, if a population has made peace with some degree of

[11] The conflict between Israel and the Palestinians is one of many modern examples. No doubt there are injustices on both sides. It would be impossible to resolve all of the claims each side could make. If this were, or continued to be, a precondition for establishing peace between the two peoples, then peace will forever be impossible. The only way forward is to establish a foundation of forgiveness and good will, which would make it possible to achieve a modicum of justice—enough to sustain peace.

progressivity in income taxation, or with a lack of progressivity in excise taxation, then it can be taken to be just as a practical matter.[12]

The third tool is a consistent statement that the allocation of burdens should take into account the ability of households to pay the amount demanded.[13] This "ability to pay" principle undoubtedly has its roots in the conviction that it is unjust to deprive anyone of the resources essential for life.[14] While citizens have a duty to pay taxes, some are rightly relieved of this burden if they cannot discharge it without failing in more fundamental obligations to care for life and health. As a practical matter, this has usually translated into entirely excusing some persons from the duty to pay and partially excusing others. We might call this a principle of mercy.

---

12 Often enough, there are persons who refuse to accept a compromise, or who enter a situation long after the fact and demand that it be renegotiated. One is reminded of the comment by Chesterton that the only person who should be allowed to move a fence is one who understands why it was put there in the first place. In many cases, a refusal to tolerate a rough approximation of justice that satisfies most people in a community will itself be a source of disharmony and injustice.

13 See, for example, Pope St. John XXIII, *Mater et Magistra* (1961), no. 132. Adam Smith invoked a similar principle: "The subjects of every state ought to contribute towards the support of government, as nearly as possible, in proportion to their respective abilities." *An Inquiry into the Nature and Causes of the Wealth of Nations*, ed. Edwin Cannan (1904), bk. 5, chap. 2, pt. 2, para. 1. Library of Economics and Liberty, http://www.econlib.org/library/Smith/smWN21.html,

14 For example, see Exodus 22:25–26 on the injustice of demanding as collateral the cloak that the borrower requires to keep warm. See also Matthew 5:42; Luke 6:30; and 1 Timothy 6:18–19; which encourage generous giving to those in need.

But this is only one way of understanding the principle. While for the most part, the Church uses the principle to justify reducing burdens on the poor, many other thinkers use it as a principle to justify increasing burdens on the wealthy (or perhaps also on the nonpoor), whether as a means of enhancing revenue or to redistribute wealth.[15] We might think of it as a principle of convenience (for the state at least). The fact remains, however, that the American people have peacefully accepted the double progressivity of our income tax policies as a principle for determining, at least in a rough way, what an individual's share of the burden ought to be. It is less clear that they are comfortable with progressivity at the higher end as a tool of redistribution (nor is it clear that it effectively functions for that purpose).

With regard to indiscriminate taxes, the situation is more complicated. Some indiscriminate taxes, such as payroll taxes (Social Security and Medicare), are payments for benefits that taxpayers expect to receive in the future, and the equality of rate may be justified on that basis. Other taxes, as for example tax on gasoline, contribute to the maintenance of roads and other aspects of public transportation. The amount of gasoline used is a reasonable, if rough, estimate of the benefit received. Excise taxes on tobacco and alcohol are partly regulatory (to discourage use) and partly opportunistic. (That is, government collects the tax because it can.) These are harder to justify as contributions to general revenue or as compensation for harmful externalities.

---

15 See the United States Conference of Catholic Bishops' pastoral letter, *Economic Justice for All* (1986), no. 202: "the tax system should be structured according to the principle of progressivity, so that those with relatively greater financial resources pay a higher rate of taxation. The inclusion of such a principle in tax policies is an important means of reducing the severe inequalities of income and wealth in the nation."

It is still harder to justify the regressive nature of sales taxes, on which states and municipalities have come to rely more heavily. The regressivity is mitigated somewhat in many jurisdictions by excluding basic commodities (e.g., food, clothing), but it remains the case that this form of tax disproportionately affects persons and households with lower incomes.

XI Minimizing Tax Liability: Evasion, Avoidance, and Mitigation

One of the most vexing ethical questions concerning taxation has to do with whether, how, and to what extent taxpayers may act to reduce or minimize the amount they are obligated to pay. There are three general avenues down which taxpayers may proceed. They may seek to *evade* the duty, in whole or in part, which entails violating the law in some respect and which we will stipulate is unethical in every instance.[1] Or they may seek to *mitigate* the duty by responding to incentives provided by law, such as charitable giving, thus effectively reducing the income subject to the levy. We will stipulate that mitigation, by definition, is morally permissible. But there is a third option, less clearly defined than the other two, that is commonly called *avoidance*. The boundaries of avoidance are blurry. Some writers think that many forms of avoidance are formally indistinguishable from evasion (having the same objective even if the means employed are not strictly illegal) but that some, at least, are much the same as mitigation (though exploiting ambiguity in the law for ends the law never intended). Other writers are inclined to

1 This assumes that the tax laws are reasonably just. Evasion often involves deception of some sort but it may also involve nothing more than a deliberate failure to file a required return.

think that anything that is not unambiguously mitigation is immoral, whether legally permitted or not.

Even on the level of general principle there is disagreement. Some authorities insist that, while taxpayers have a duty to contribute to society and to obey tax laws, they are not prohibited from seeking to lower the amount they are bound to pay.[2] Others insist that there is no such right, or if there is, it is limited to cases where the law provides an incentive, in the form of a reduction in tax, to act in a certain way (e.g., making charitable contributions). Apart from this, seeking to reduce tax obligations is usually, if not always, an effort to escape paying one's fair share. Of course, an army of lawyers and accountants have arisen to assist taxpayers to pursue this end, by means legal and creative, and sometimes by means that are only arguably not illegal.

We have observed before that the contest between taxpayer and tax collector is an ancient one that shows no signs of ending. The question about the moral permissibility of avoidance

2 Perhaps the most famous statement in support of the right of taxpayers to reduce their obligation comes from Judge Learned Hand:

> Over and over again courts have said that there is nothing sinister in so arranging one's affairs as to keep taxes as low as possible. Everybody does so, rich or poor; and all do right, for nobody owes any public duty to pay more than the law demands: taxes are enforced exactions, not voluntary contributions. To demand more in the name of morals is mere cant. *Commissioner v. Newman*, 159 F.2d 848, 851 (2d Cir. 1947)—Hand, J. dissenting.

On a previous occasion he had also said: "Any one may so arrange his affairs that his taxes shall be as low as possible; he is not bound to choose that pattern which will best pay the Treasury; there is not even a patriotic duty to increase one's taxes"—*Gregory v. Helvering*, 69 F.2d 809, 810 (2d Cir. 1934).

is just one more engagement in a very long war. My purpose in this section is to offer an analysis of the question by drawing on some of the concepts of the Catholic social tradition that we have developed.

Let me begin with a couple of general observations. First, it seems that the fact that the issue of avoidance has become so prominent in recent years is, in part, a consequence of the complexity of the tax codes of modern developed nations. This happens in two ways. On the one hand, in seeking to use the tax code to raise revenue, regulate behaviors, and redistribute wealth, states pursue goals that are sometimes incompatible.[3] In another way, legislators over the years have succumbed to so many temptations to create exceptions and preferences to the income tax codes that many of these modifications conflict with one another or create options or consequences that the legislators never imagined or intended. Yet, they are part of the code, and it is not strictly illegal in most cases for taxpayers to exploit them to their benefit.

All of this is further complicated by the lack of a common moral language with which to consider the issue. Libertarians are fond of rejecting the idea that there is a duty to pay taxes at all.[4] An opposing position sees efforts at legitimating avoidance

---

3 For example, legislators sometimes propose to raise tax rates on the wealthy, allegedly as a matter of fairness, even though they know very well that a rise in rates may lower overall revenues. On other occasions, in the United States at least, we enact tax preferences to encourage certain behaviors but then, with policies such as the Alternative Minimum Tax, we attempt to claw back revenues from taxpayers who respond to the preferences.

4 See, for example, Tibor R. Machan, "Taxation: The Ethics of Its Avoidance or Dodging," in *Contemporary Readings in Law and Social Justice* 2 (2010): 80–91. He writes: "It is clear that taxation is extortion and has no place, any more than serfdom, in a just legal order," 87.

as an assault on the common good.[5] Furthermore, some writers subscribe to one version or another of ethical deontology, while others are utilitarians, legal positivists, or proponents of still other ethical schools—each with differing foundational assumptions and conceptual frameworks. Among them, there is often no commonly accepted rationale for obedience to the law at all.

The result of all this is a complex stew of laws and theories, values and objectives. It is complicated enough when we deal merely with individuals and households; the complexity and intensity are greatly multiplied when multinational corporations are involved with many billions of dollars at stake and the tax codes of multiple nations in tension.

Clearly, we will not resolve all of these issues here, nor am I concerned with offering criticism of the various opposing legal and philosophical positions. Instead, as in other cases, I think the Catholic social tradition can be an effective lens to allow us to see how some resolutions might be crafted.

We should begin with the reminder that human beings are social creatures whose well-being and fulfillment are intimately connected with our participation in communities ranging from families to societies. Following from this, we have a fundamental duty, in *general* justice, to contribute to the common goods of our communities. That is, each of these communities has a set of claims on us, even prior to the creation of a set of human laws. But communities require authority, they require someone to direct the actions of the members to common goods. As a

[5] See William B. Barker, "The Ideology of Tax Avoidance," *Loyola University of Chicago Law Review* 40 (2009): 229–51. Barker writes: "Tax law's domain is not simply the domain of the finite words of the statute. The tax law is a totality of language, purposes and intent that aims to achieve certain social goals … the liberal ideology of individual rights [supporting avoidance] robs these values of their full normative force," 250–51.

practical matter, communities cannot survive without such authority. One of the responsibilities of civil authority is to define and enact positive laws for the community. The duty to do this well, and in conformity with the natural law, falls on these authorities as a matter of *legal* justice. Reciprocally, the members of the community have a duty, also in *legal* justice, to obey the just laws of the society, among which are laws concerning taxation.

The laws enacted by civil authorities make the requirements of general justice concrete and specific. To put it another way, prior to the enactment of civil laws (imagine a primitive society), there is a duty to support the common good but no duty to pay taxes. Only with the enactment of pertinent civil laws does the duty to pay taxes, in such and such an amount, on such a date, to such an official, actually arise. This leads us to the issue of a "fair share."

Is There Such a Thing as a "Fair Share" of the Tax Burden?

It has become commonplace in political campaigns for some candidates to demand that the wealthy begin to pay their fair share of taxes. As we noted earlier, a glance at the breakdown of income tax receipts indicates that the wealthy—however this adjective is defined—do indeed pay a disproportionate amount of their income in tax. But is it a fair share?

We agree that every citizen[6] has a duty to contribute to the support of government, and that the duty is made concrete by the action of legislatures. Absent the action of the legislature, however, there is no such thing as a fair share in the abstract. No fair share can be calculated objectively because there are no

6 Obviously some citizens (children, for example) are often exempt from the duty to pay tax.

commonly agreed on principles for doing so and no commonly agreed on priorities to determine what the needs of government are. Even if we limited our consideration to an income tax—and we know that income is difficult to define and to measure—too many unanswered questions would remain for us to calculate a fair share independently of a determination by civil authority. Does fair require absolute equality, where everyone pays the same amount (as in a sales tax)? Should such an amount be calculated per person or per household? Should fair assume a progressive structure? And if so, should we adopt single progressivity, reducing the rate for low-income taxpayers but keeping it absolutely equal for everyone over a certain minimum income? Or should we adopt dual progressivity, with lower rates for lower-income taxpayers, moderate rates for middle-income taxpayers, and much higher rates for the wealthy? What, in fact, would these rates be? What should count as income? And what deductions would we allow? Just a moment's reflection should make it clear that fairness cannot be calculated in the abstract.

But given the action of the legislature, the fair share for taxpayers is defined by law and is precisely what the law says it is. The claim that there is a fair share that can be identified independently of the law is groundless, however rhetorically appealing it may be to some.[7]

Allow me to offer a rough analogy. Suppose I agree to begin working for a company as a truck driver, and I agree to begin work on Monday morning at 8:00. Faithful to my promise, I arrive at the company's offices on time, but there is no one there

[7] The irony should not be lost on us when a member of the legislature, who shares the responsibility to set tax rates and conditions, complains that some taxpayers are failing in their duties when they comply with the law. Perhaps this could be interpreted more benignly as a complaint about other legislators who decline to vote in favor of rates that the member believes would be fair.

to tell me what truck to drive, what to load on to the truck, or where to take it. Because I have promised to do so, I have an obligation to come to work (analogous to general justice) but absent the necessary instructions, I am unable to do any work in fact. And if someone were to criticize me for not doing any productive work on my first day, that criticism would be groundless and unfair. It is the responsibility of my employer to issue instructions about what I ought to do (analogous to legal justice), and without those instructions I have no concrete duty. Similarly, the fair share any taxpayer is obligated to pay is what the law requires. If the law is ambiguous, it is not an injustice on the part of taxpayers if they interpret it in their favor; it is the duty of the legislature to remove the ambiguity as best they can, and the duty of courts to protect well-intentioned citizens.

How Far May Taxpayers Go to Minimize Their Obligations?

Only persons have rights and duties; organizations do not—though, of course, persons act for organizations and have special duties and rights as members of organizations. The paradigm case of a taxpayer, therefore, is the individual (or the household). We will begin our consideration there before moving on to corporations as taxpayers.

As we have said, the individual has a duty in *general* justice to support the common good, which translates more practically into a stable inclination to act for the common good as opportunities arise (formalized and perfected as the virtue of solidarity). This inclination is made concrete by acts of legislators, specifying what members of the community are to do. Such specifications include everything from traffic rules to military service to paying taxes. It is crucial to remember that members of the community, under the jurisdiction of civil authorities, have a duty to submit to just laws—and indeed, a duty to assume that the laws are just unless strong reasons to the contrary are presented.

As a consequence, it is a mistake, from the perspective of the Catholic social tradition, to assume that taxpayers and civil authorities are locked in a contest in which civil authorities seek to acquire as much wealth as they can from taxpayers, and taxpayers rightly seek to minimize their payments as much as possible without incurring penalties. Instead, it is more appropriate to see the relationship as peaceful and ordered to the common good, as much as are traffic regulations or other principles of good social order.

In the case of many sorts of tax levies, there is little room for dispute. A sales tax is a fixed percentage of a purchase price; there is nothing to contest. I might disagree with the value that the assessor assigns to my home, and I can appeal that valuation, but beyond that, again, there is nothing to contest. Something similar can be said for tariffs and excise taxes. But when we come to the income tax, there is a wide range of variables open to dispute. What can individuals do and not do?

First, though it probably goes without saying, deliberate misrepresentation of the nature, amount, or timing of income is impermissible. No taxpayer can rightly conceal income that would otherwise be subject to taxation. Believing that the rate in force is too high or that certain irregular deductions from income should be permitted are not valid reasons for lying (for this is what it would be) about income. Neither is disagreement with government policies and programs a valid reason for withholding tax payments.[8]

[8] We might take a different view if the government itself were illegitimate or widely engaged in deeply immoral activities (which would itself call into questions its legitimacy). Even in such a case, while an individual might be objectively justified in protesting government actions by withholding tax payments, he or she would

But setting aside deliberate deception still leaves open a set of other options. Tax codes in developed countries (which are often mimicked in less developed countries) typically contain an array of incentives, preferences, and definitions. Some of these are intended indirectly to support taxpayer activities that the state should be interested to foster, such as a deduction from taxable income for dependent care. Others, of course, promote special interests and still others are efforts to recognize a variety of special circumstances that affect the definition of income. It is often possible to claim a benefit deriving from one of these preferences even though the situation an individual is in may be very different from what the law anticipated.[9]

Some would say that individuals are at liberty to do anything within the law (that is, anything that is not a clear violation of the letter of the law) to reduce their tax obligations. I think that the Catholic tradition would not entirely agree. Taxpayers should be entitled to mitigate their obligations within the law,

still be subject to penalties for doing so, in fact if not in justice. In any event, the tradition of the Church is very reluctant to support revolutionary activities.

9 Some scholars on this point wish to invoke what they refer to as the "spirit" of the law, which might be what some or all of the legislators intended to achieve in voting for a particular preference. They claim that it is immoral to violate the spirit of the law and that courts should enforce the spirit against instances where someone has abided by the letter of the law while offending the spirit. It is perilous to proceed down this path, even if a few examples make it appealing. In general, the tradition of the Church, most clearly evidenced in the arena of canon law but applicable to civil law as well, is that it is the text of the law that binds. There may be a legislative backstory that clarifies the intentions of legislators, and this backstory may be used to address ambiguities, but where the text is clear, the alleged spirit cannot be used as a sort of super-principle to justify punishing some instances of literal compliance. The duty of clarity falls on legislators.

but general justice would constrain the degree to which they can exploit ambiguities or loopholes, which are inevitable in a highly complex tax code.

Though its conclusions are not entirely consistent with the Catholic social tradition (nor do they purport to be), an article by Zoe and John Prebble about an enterprising farmer in New Zealand shows how tax law might be manipulated. The farmer's land comprised six fields, each of which was of relatively poor soil, so poor that each field was left to pasture for five out of six years. The farmer planted one field each year, which was the most profitable part of the farm. But then he did more:

> The taxpayer established a trust with his wife and children as beneficiaries. Each year he let the current cropping field to the trust at a low rental. The trust engaged him as a contractor to sow the field in wheat and then to harvest it. The profits went to the trust. In respect of that field the taxpayer derived only rent and fees for his work. The rotation was repeated from year to year. The taxpayer thus reduced his income and incidence of tax. The trust was taxed each year for the income derived from the cropping field but at a lower rate than the taxpayer would have suffered.[10]

As it happens, New Zealand had an anti-avoidance provision in law at the time, and the farmer's plan was disallowed. For our purposes, however, it illustrates how otherwise neutral provisions in the law can be exploited in such a way as to misrepresent the real nature of a situation. I submit that such misrepresentations, while they may not strictly violate the law, nevertheless seek to present a reality as something different from what it is and therefore constitute an unethical means of reducing a tax obligation. Or to put it another way, taxpayers

[10] See Zoe Prebble and John Prebble, "The Morality of Tax Avoidance," *Creighton Law Review* 43 (2010): 693–745, at 709.

have a duty to represent their situations fairly—in terms favorable to themselves where there is legitimate ambiguity—and to accept the obligation that follows. To create illusory or sham legal structures, which may not be illegal in themselves, is to violate one's duty of legal justice.[11]

How Far May Corporations Go to Minimize Their Tax Obligations?

For purposes of ethical analysis, the situation of for-profit corporations as taxpayers is a subset of the case of individual taxpayers. Corporations do not pay taxes; shareholders do (by surrendering some of the profits that would otherwise accrue to their holdings). Corporations do not have rights and duties; shareholders, boards, and managers do.[12]

---

[11] There is also reason to suggest that schemes to exploit features of the law in general and the tax code in particular are in some sense a response to an exceedingly complicated and often burdensome system of taxation. I mentioned earlier that we need not assume that government's interests are identical with government's needs. To take the ever-growing preferences of government for revenue as an objective need that must be satisfied is also to create the inclination to regard a great many of the activities of citizens as taxable objects and improperly to regard their wealth as the wealth (that is, the property) of the nation.

[12] There is a lively discussion to be had about the wisdom of levying taxes against corporations rather than against shareholders directly. In my judgment, the Catholic social tradition has no position on this question and legislators are free to do as they please, which in most cases is to tax corporations. In doing so, they certainly have popular support and often unfairly complain that corporations do not pay their fair share. Questions should be raised about whether taxing corporations, which are in a position to pass their costs on to customers, employees, and others in a way that individuals are not, serves the common good well.

Obviously, the situation of corporations is generally much more complicated than that of individuals, though the moral principles involved are much the same. Of course, the sums of money involved in specific cases are far larger than would be involved with individuals. For this and other reasons, it is more rewarding for governments to press corporations for tax payments and more rewarding for corporations to resist as creatively as possible. (Corporations also have resources on a scale unavailable to individuals.)

While corporate boards and managers have a duty to shareholders to manage in their best interests, they do not, strictly speaking, have a legal duty to maximize shareholder wealth. Despite some common confusion about this, the fact is that boards and managers have no warrant to do for shareholders (as taxpayers) what it would be unethical for the shareholders (as taxpayers) to do for themselves. Therefore, if it would be wrong for individual taxpayers to misrepresent their situations in order to reduce their tax obligations, it would also be wrong for managers to do so. In particular, it would be wrong for boards and managers to take advantage of wrinkles in the law, whether in one nation or across multiple national boundaries, to engage in sham transactions, adopt fictitious structures, and so forth in order to present a smaller taxable profile to the authorities.

Opportunities to engage in legal misrepresentations abound.[13] Many of these opportunities are presented by the failure of governments to collaborate in moderating tax pressures and in

---

[13] Though I disagree with elements of their analysis, an interesting account of some contemporary strategies is Rafael Bellaver and Pedro Henrique Chaves Araujo, "Ethical Dimensions of International Tax Planning," Bloomberg BNA, *Daily Tax Report*, 198 DTR J-1, 13 October 2016. Available at SSRN: https://ssrn.com/abstract=2855999.

regularizing tax policies to reduce both perverse incentives and loopholes, though efforts move forward slowly to achieve this.

In sum, the fair burden on taxpayers is determined by the action of legislatures. Apart from the enactment of tax codes, no objective fair share can be calculated. Individuals and corporations (whose boards and managers act for individual shareholders) have a duty in legal justice to obey the law and pay the taxes the law requires of them. This means refraining from using legal means to misrepresent their status. At the same time, they have no duty to pay more than the law requires and may freely seek to reduce their tax obligations through legal means that do not misrepresent realities.

XII Conclusion

In this small volume, I have tried, first, to clarify some foundational concepts in Catholic moral theology and the social tradition, and second, to apply those concepts, with support from documents in the tradition, to questions concerning taxation. Now, as a summary of sorts, I want to consider a few things that the tradition teaches us—and does not teach us—about the levying of taxes.

We should not assume, in pursuing these reflections, that the Catholic social tradition maps neatly onto contemporary partisan politics or secular philosophies. It does not. There may be some correspondence here and there, and some Catholic voices who energetically support a particular partisan position in its entirety, but the comprehensive Catholic vision is not equivalent to any secular view.

What the Tradition Teaches Us

First, the Catholic social tradition teaches us that, as images of God, the natural flourishing of human persons consists in the full exercise of our capacities to reason well, to act for the good, and to participate in civic friendship. As a consequence, the common good of society, the protection and improvement of which is the reason for the existence of the state, consists in those conditions that would make it possible for each and every person in the community to flourish. It does not and cannot consist in making individuals passive recipients of the material requirements of a decent life. Of course, as embodied spirits, we do need material goods, but an essential part of our well-being involves acquiring these goods for ourselves and our families through productive work. The state can assist us in becoming self-reliant and self-determining—as social beings, not as isolated individuals—but it cannot do this for us or to us. As a result, the state must respect a very large zone of social life, a rich assemblage of families and associations that it may nurture but ought not to control. This acts as a natural limit on state activity and on the need for tax revenues.

Second, the Catholic social tradition teaches us that individuals and families have a natural right to own property privately. It is in recognizing this right that the Catholic social tradition reveals one of its most distinctive features: the emphasis on the family as the foundational element of society. Indeed, on the Catholic view, the family precedes the state, has rights and an independence that is prior to and not a gift of the state, and ought to be served by the state. The right of private ownership, which is also not a creature of the state (though, again, the state has a duty to respect, govern, and protect it), is justified in part by the needs of the family. The wealth of a society is an aggregate measure, for the most part, of wealth owned privately by individuals and families; it is not the possession of the state. Nevertheless, the state has a claim on some amount of private property in order to perform its proper functions, and it claims this amount through laws levying taxes.

Third, the Catholic social tradition teaches us that members of a society have a duty to support the common good in various ways, not least by peacefully paying just taxes. Members of a society have a duty in justice to support the common good. This duty is both general, which requires that members incline themselves to act for the common good as opportunities arise, and concrete (i.e., legal). This abstract duty is made concrete by just laws enacted by legitimate civil authority. One of the most common and important categories of these laws concerns the levying of taxes. Unless there is an unambiguous demonstration to the contrary, individuals are obliged, in justice, to regard tax laws as just and to obey in letter and spirit.

Fourth, the Catholic social tradition teaches us that the burden of taxation should be proportioned to the ability of individuals and households to pay. For the most part, just taxation will take into account the ability of individuals and families to bear the burden demanded. In particular, they should not be required to pay taxes out of funds they absolutely need to sustain a minimally decent life. This principle encourages some degree of progressivity in taxation, especially where the object of taxation is income. It is less clear that the tradition holds that the wealthy (however that is defined) must be required to pay a disproportionately higher rate of tax than the majority of the population. Furthermore, the thrust of the tradition is in favor of lower rather than higher levels of taxation so that individuals and families retain more of their money and can more effectively serve their communities through acts of charity and generosity.

Fifth, the Catholic social tradition teaches us that the people of particular nations are free to make determinations about what operations to delegate to government and what forms of taxation, consistent with natural justice, the community will employ to collect revenue. There is, in other words, no perfect form of taxation, no ideal level of taxation, no object of taxation that is ruled out in principle. Some tax levies may certainly be unjust in their details but apart from this, a community is free to adopt whatever forms it prefers that can be accepted peacefully. Of course, it also follows that no form, no level, no object, and no target group will be necessary in a just program of taxation.

What the Tradition Does *Not* Teach Us

First, the Catholic social tradition does *not* teach us that all social issues should be addressed through government action (though certainly some should be so addressed). The tradition understands society to be a much larger association than the state. Think of the analogy of a human body. The heart and lungs are indispensable, but they are not the whole body. Other organs do things that the heart and lungs cannot, with each organ making its own contribution to the well-being of the whole body. Similarly, the state has a role to play in supporting the health and integrity of the society but so do the family and a rich collection of intermediate associations. Communities are free to delegate functions to the state but the Church has long been cautious about delegating too much. It recognizes the importance of the intermediate bodies, not only in terms of their efficiency and their proximity to the problems but also in terms of the importance to individuals of the exercise of charity. Whatever government may do, however dedicated and professional its employees, it cannot substitute for charity nor can Christians hire it out. The general posture of the Church has been to recognize a role for government in addressing social issues—a role that may naturally be larger in more complicated communities—but at the same time to want to protect a sphere of action for private associations.

Second, the Catholic social tradition does *not* teach us that larger, more comprehensive government is to be preferred. Any number of thinkers in the twentieth century commented on the tendency for government to trend toward totalitarianism. By this they did not mean that government tended to become dictatorial or fascist. They simply observed an inclination for government to insert itself into more and more areas of private life to exercise regulatory functions and perhaps even to criminalize what previously had been regarded as private behaviors, however rude or offensive. In many respects, the Church has been careful about supporting the growth of government, often justifying government intervention in cases of crisis but warning that the intervention ought to cease when the crisis is resolved. All of this is a reflection of the Church's concern with subsidiarity, which requires respect for the proper functions of the various organs of society. Our experience in history is that the more powerful organs have a tendency to absorb the functions of those smaller and less powerful. We are particularly concerned to protect the integrity of the family. While government can do many things well, and people increasingly look to government to address large problems, there is a reciprocal principle that tells us we should also observe boundaries to the growth of government operations and responsibilities. On the other side of these boundaries lie the many functions of private organizations.

Third, the Catholic social tradition does *not* teach us that wealth ought to be redistributed through taxation. Pope Leo XIII explicitly rejected the socialist description of society as composed of classes who were natural enemies to one another. Instead, he acknowledged that there are many forms of inequality that are natural, and these natural differences give rise to different groupings within society. Nevertheless, we are all children of the same God and these differences should not be obstacles to civic friendship. The key is to embrace the concept of vocation. That is, every person is called to make some contribution to the community, to serve some purpose. Those with greater talents, opportunities, and good fortune, have proportionately greater responsibilities to contribute to society. The wealthy may be fortunate in one sense, but they have a solemn duty to use their wealth well. One of the functions of the Church is persistently to remind people of their duties to society. To use taxation as a vehicle for distribution, however, is to neglect this dimension. That the wealthy have resources is one thing; what they do with their resources is quite another—and is really the important thing. For the Church, the goal is not to equalize wealth in society but to encourage that wealth be used—generally by private initiative—for the common good. This is not to deny a role for government but to balance that role against the importance of private beneficence.

Fourth, the Catholic social tradition does *not* teach us that the needs of the poor take priority over all other items in government budgets. To be sure, care for the poor is an inescapable Christian duty, but the impact of budgets on the poor is not the only moral measure to be employed. We need to begin by being clear about what we mean by an impact on the poor. We could consider budgetary decisions that directly harm the poor and seek to avoid those in every instance. Or, which may be more common, we could consider programs for the poor that we choose not to fund in favor of other programs that require support. Every dollar of a government budget that we spend on the poor is a dollar not spent on education, infrastructure, policing, public health, or some other critical function. The Catholic social tradition requires the state to support the common good as a whole; it does not require the state to subordinate all functional areas to any single issue—even the situation of the poor. Furthermore, the public definition of poverty tends to be in terms of sufficiency of material resources, and government programs are geared toward addressing insufficiencies. But, as St. Teresa of Calcutta reminded us, the most terrible anguish is not physical poverty or material deprivation—though this in itself can be a very bad thing—it is the anguish of not being wanted; of being rejected, neglected, and forgotten; of being alone. Given their nature, government programs, regardless of their size, cannot address this dimension of poverty. This really belongs to the private sector, to person-to-person contact, and to the ministry of the churches. Once again, government has a role to play, but it also has many proper responsibilities and cannot neglect them to focus on just one. In a free society, citizens, at their best, freely attend to needs in their own communities and are supported in doing this when taxation is light enough to allow them to bring their own resources to bear.

* * *

Tax policies and tax levies are an unavoidable part of civilized life. The social tradition of the Church emphasizes the duty of citizens to support their government as well as the duties of civil authorities to govern wisely and to respect the ownership rights of individuals and families. The goal in all of this is the promotion of the common good, which requires prudence and balance. This is not easy to achieve and to sustain—but it is worth the struggle.

Bibliography

Papal Encyclicals and Other Church Documents

Pope Leo XIII (1878–1903).

Diuturnum (On Civil Government), 1881.

Immortale Dei (On the Christian Constitution of States), 1885.

Rerum Novarum (On the Condition of Workers), 1891.

Pope Pius XI (1922–1939).

Quadragesimo Anno (On Reconstruction of the Social Order), 1931.

Pope St. John XXIII (1958–1963).

Mater et Magistra (On Christianity and Social Progress), 1961.

Pacem in Terris (On Peace and Human Rights), 1963.

Pope Paul VI (1963–1978).

Populorum Progressio (On the Development of Peoples), 1967.

Pope St. John Paul II (1978–2005).

Sollicitudo Rei Socialis (On International Development), 1987.

Centesimus Annus (On Human Persons and the Economy), 1991.

Pope Benedict XVI (2005–2013).

Deus Caritas Est (On Love and Social Justice), 2005.

Caritas in Veritate (On Love, Truth and Development), 2009.

Second Vatican Council, *Gaudium et Spes* (Pastoral Constitution on the Church in the Modern World), 1965.

National Conference of Catholic Bishops, *Economic Justice for All*, 1986.

Pontifical Council for Justice and Peace, *Compendium of the Social Doctrine of the Church*, 2004.

Further Reading

Blum, Walter J., and Harry Kalven. "The Uneasy Case for Progressive Taxation." Chicago: University of Chicago Press, 1953. Reprint of an earlier article: *University of Chicago Law Review* 19 (1952): 417–520.

Burke, Thomas Patrick. *The Concept of Justice: Is Social Justice Just?* New York: Continuum, 2011.

Cook, Louis H. "Backgrounds of Modern Taxation." *Taxes: The Tax Magazine* 30 (1952): 627–37.

Crowe, Martin T. *The Moral Obligation of Paying Just Taxes*. CUA Studies in Sacred Theology 84. Washington, DC: Catholic University of America Press, 1944.

Curran, Charles E. "Just Taxation in the Roman Catholic Tradition." *Journal of Religious Ethics* 13, no. 1 (1985): 113–33.

de Jouvenal, Bertrand. *The Ethics of Redistribution*. Cambridge: Cambridge University Press, 1952.

Fagan, Elmer D. "Recent and Contemporary Theories of Progressive Taxation." *Journal of Political Economy* 46, no. 4 (1938): 457–98.

Groves, Harold M. *Tax Philosophers: Two Hundred Years of Thought in Great Britain and the United States*. Edited by Donald J. Curran. Madison: University of Wisconsin Press, 1974.

Holmes, Stephen, and Cass R. Sunstein, *The Cost of Rights: Why Liberty Depends on Taxes*. New York: W. W. Norton and Co., 1999.

Lee, R. Alton. *A History of Regulatory Taxation*. Lexington: University of Kentucky Press, 1973.

Liberatore, Matteo. *Principles of Political Economy*. Translated by Edward Heneage Dering. New York: Benziger, 1891.

Machan, Tibor. "Taxation: The Ethics of Its Avoidance and Dodging." *Contemporary Readings in Law and Social Justice* 2 (2010): 80–91.

Meredith, Christopher T. "The Ethical Basis for Taxation in the Thought of Thomas Aquinas." *Journal of Markets and Morality* 11, no. 1 (2008): 41–57.

Meredith, Christopher T. "Taxation and Legal Plunder in the Thought of Frederic Bastiat." *Journal of Markets and Morality* 12, no. 2 (2009): 297–314.

Mellon, Andrew W. *Taxation: The Peoples' Business*. New York: Macmillan, 1924.

Murphy, Liam, and Thomas Nagel. *The Myth of Ownership*. Oxford: Oxford University Press, 2002.

Musgrave, Richard A., and Alan T. Peacock, eds. *Classics in the Theory of Public Finance*. New York: Macmillan, 1967.

Nozick, Robert. *Anarchy, State, and Utopia*. New York: Basic Books, 1974.

Prebble, Zoë, and John Prebble. "The Morality of Tax Avoidance." *Creighton Law Review* 43 (2010): 693–745.

Ryan, John A. *Distributive Justice*, 3rd ed. New York: Macmillan, 1942.

Rothbard, Murray N. "The Uneasy Case for Degressive Taxation: A Critique of Blum and Kalven." *Quarterly Journal of Austrian Economics* 4, no. 1 (2001): 43–61.

Seligman, Edwin R. A. *Essays in Taxation*. New York: Macmillan, 1921.

Thorndike, Joseph J., and Dennis J. Ventry, eds. *Tax Justice: The Ongoing Debate*. Washington, DC: Urban Institute Press, 2002.

Webber, Carolyn, and Aaron Wildavsky. *A History of Taxation and Expenditure in the Western World*. New York: Simon and Schuster, 1986.

Yu, Dennis J. *Render to Caesar? The Morality of Taxation*. Makati City, Philippines: St. Pauls, 2016.

About the Author

Robert G. Kennedy is professor and former chair of the Department of Catholic Studies at the University of St. Thomas in St. Paul, Minnesota, where he was also for many years a professor of management. He is the author of a number of essays, book reviews, and articles on topics such as professionalism, business ethics, and ethical investment, as well as on issues related to culture, public life, and the Catholic social tradition. He is a named contributor to *A Reflection on the Vocation of the Business Leader*, a document published in 2012 by the Pontifical Council for Justice and Peace. His previous contribution to the Acton Institute's Christian Social Thought Series is *The Good That Business Does* (2006; Italian translation, 2014).

Kennedy holds master's degrees in biblical criticism and business administration. He received his PhD in medieval studies from the University of Notre Dame, where his dissertation advisor was Ralph McInerny.

Made in the USA
Monee, IL
04 November 2026

67377496R00079